Leadership across Cultures

New Horizons in Management Sciences

Edited by Lukasz Sulkowski

Volume 10

PETER LANG

Jerzy Mączyński, Łukasz Sułkowski
Sylwia Przytuła (eds.)

Leadership across Cultures

PETER LANG

Bibliographic Information published by the Deutsche Nationalbibliothek
The Deutsche Nationalbibliothek lists this publication in the Deutsche Nationalbibliografie; detailed bibliographic data is available in the internet at http://dnb.d-nb.de.

Library of Congress Cataloging-in-Publication Data
A CIP catalog record for this book has been applied for at the Library of Congress.

This publication was financially supported by the University of Social Sciences, Poland.

Printed by CPI books GmbH, Leck

ISSN 2194-153X
ISBN 978-3-631-79318-3 (Print)
E-ISBN 978-3-631-79773-0 (E-Book)
E-ISBN978-3-631-79774-7 (EPUB)
E-ISBN 978-3-631-79775-4 (MOBI)
DOI 10.3726/b15974

Peter Lang – Berlin · Bern · Bruxelles · New York · Oxford · Warszawa · Wien

This publication has been peer reviewed.
www.peterlang.com

Preface

Leadership in organizations has become a significant topic in scientific research over the last few decades. Bass (1990) and Yukl (2002) provide overviews of the extensive literature developed over the years. Nevertheless, an area where new developments in leadership investigations are needed are cross-cultural studies. Under the GLOBE project, developed by Robert House (Professor of Wharton School at the University of Pennsylvania) and designed to fill this gap, "leadership was defined as the ability to motivate, influence and enable individuals to contribute to the objectives of organizations of which they are members" (House, et al. 2004, p. XXII).

Although our monograph is primarily aimed at academics, it contains valuable information relevant to leaders engaged in cross-border interactions. The information resulting from the research presented in this book can be applied as a guide for managers from different cultures interacting with each other. Currently there is a great need for effective international cooperation, not only for the effective practice of leadership, but also for the advancement of human prosperity. The main purpose of this book is to analyze particular cross-cultural aspects of leadership effectiveness.

This book is a product of the collective efforts of 13 scholars from different universities in Poland and Austria. The first chapter, developed by Dariusz Doliński and Tomasz Grzyb titled ***Social Influence in Management – Possibilities for Using the "Power WE" in the Everyday Work of a Manager***, deals with considerations concerning the rule called "the Power of WE" in the social activities of a manager. Additionally, they analyze the role of the culture in which such activities are performed. At the same time, they provide strong arguments that the need for belonging to a group, the need to consider themselves and other people in terms of "We" is universal, and should be beneficial to managers around the world.

The second chapter, prepared by Czesław Sikorski, deals with **leaderless organization**. The author stressed the idea that the role of a contemporary leader requires a fundamental change in the relationship between the manager and his followers. Supervision should be concerned with developing and applying the potential of employees for the effectiveness of organization. Therefore, it is necessary to develop such a model of leadership in which the supervisor treats his followers as partners with whom she/he solves organizational problems collectively.

Auer-Rizzi et al., in their chapter titled ***Social Partnership: Comparisons between Managers in Four Countries Based on the Vroom/Yetton Model***, analyze the problem of mean level of participation (MLP), the rate of agreement with the feasible set, and the violation rate of quality rules and acceptance rules based on a comparison of managers from Austria, Germany, Czech Republic, and Poland.

Łukasz Sułkowski, in his chapter titled ***Academic Leadership in University Mergers***, expressed the view that academic leadership should encourage organizational members to function together, leading to the fulfillment of the objectives of institutions of science and higher education. The concept of effective academic leadership is analyzed from managerial, psychological, and sociological perspectives.

Łukasz Haromszeki and Tadeusz Listwan, in their chapter ***Organizational Leaders in Public Institutions***, analyze research of organizational cultures that are preferred by leaders in public institutions. Specifically their chapter identifies and presents significant aspects of the organizational culture that dominates public institutions where opinions and ideas about the specifics of future leadership relationships are discussed. According to the authors, in public organizations of the future the following elements should be included: a forward way of thinking, the reduction of formalization and the application of the project approach, applying new solutions in the field of employee development, arranging creative motivational systems, and strengthening the culture of cooperation, all of which have the capacity to result in increased efficiency in task realization.

Michał Chmielecki in his chapter titled ***Leading the Eastern Way: Chinese Philosophy, Culture and Innovation*** analyzes the successful transformation of economic growth in China. He stresses the idea that it would not be easy to select a country that has successfully performed such a radical transformation in such a short period of time. For the last 30 years, China has emerged as a key player in the global economy. In the recent international financial crisis and recession China performed better than western countries.

The Chinese government is currently developing programs to gain technological advantages in clean energy, supercomputers, medicine, and national defense, among other areas.

Sylwia Przytuła, in her chapter entitled ***Expatriate Leaders***, discusses the process of international mobility of enterprises and their expansion into foreign markets. Since managers around the globe increasingly face the challenges presented to them through different cultural organizations with divergent expectations about power and interpersonal relations, it becomes significant for them to understand how these differences can influence effective leadership.

Additionally, the author reviews literature on "global leadership" and "expatriate management", in order to identify crucial competencies for expatriate leaders in response to the growing demand of such international managers.

Finally, Jerzy Mączyński and Łukasz Sułkowski, in their chapter ***A Seven Nation Study of Leadership Attributes***, analyze the empirical findings concerning a cross-cultural investigation of traits and behaviors, comparing a representative sample of Polish middle managers with a representative sample of chief executive officers from six chosen countries (USA, Austria, Germany, China, Taiwan, and Russia). The authors provide research evidence that the investigated chief executive officers from the above countries (with the exception of Russian CEOs and Polish middle managers) were positively evaluated by their followers in regard to: inspirational, visionary, integrity, performance-oriented leadership behaviors, team-oriented behavior, and participative leadership style.

We are grateful to all the outstanding authors for their contributions reflected in this book, and we thank them for all their efforts in preparing inspiring chapters, which we acknowledge with gratitude. We are also grateful to *John Wolf*, a California native with a master's degree in applied linguistics, who helped ensure that the level of English in the chapters is at the highest level. A very special thanks goes to *Anna Mączyńska* – the daughter of the first editor of this book – for her considerate and invaluable assistance in e-mail correspondence with the co-authors of the present monograph.

Our final conclusion is that, hopefully, in this book we were able to make a relevant contribution to the organizational behavior, and leadership literature. The knowledge contained in our book will also provide a rich source of information for anyone interested in doing business across borders.

Jerzy Mączyński
Łukasz Sułkowski
Sylwia Przytuła

References

Bass, B.M. (1990). *Bass and Stogdill's handbook of leadership: theory, research, and managerial applications, 3-rd ed.* New York: Free Press.

House, R.J., et al. (2004). *Culture, leadership, and organizations. The GLOBE study of 62 societies. Thousand Oaks, London, New Delhi: Sage Publications.*

Yukl, G.A. (2002). *Leadership in organizations, 5-th ed. Upper Saddle River: Prentice Hall.*

Contents

List of Contributors 11

Dariusz Doliński and Tomasz Grzyb
Social Influence in Management – Possibilities for Using the "Power of WE" in the Everyday Work of a Manager 13

Czesław Sikorski
Leaderless Organization or Organization of Leaders 27

Werner Auer-Rizzi, Gerhard Reber, Jerzy Mączyński, Łukasz Prysiński, and Dariusz Wyspiański
Social Partnership: Comparisons between Managers in Four Countries Based on the Vroom/Yetton Model 55

Łukasz Sułkowski
Academic Leadership in University Mergers 75

Łukasz Haromszeki and Tadeusz Listwan
Organisational Leaders in Public Institutions: Operating Amidst the Prevalent and Desirable Organisational Culture 89

Michał Chmielecki
Leading the Eastern Way: Chinese Philosophy and Innovation 109

Sylwia Przytuła
Expatriate Leaders 121

Jerzy Mączyński and Łukasz Sułkowski
A Seven-Nation Study of Leadership Attributes 151

List of Illustrations 169

List of Tables 171

About the Authors 173

List of Contributors

Werner Auer-Rizzi and Gerhard Reber
Johannes Kepler University of Linz, Austria

Michał Chmielecki
University of Social Sciences, Łódź, Poland

Dariusz Dolinski and Tomasz Grzyb
SWPS University of Social Sciences and Humanities, Faculty in Wrocław, Poland

Łukasz Haromszeki and Tadeusz Listwan
Wrocław University of Economics, Poland

Jerzy Mączyński, Łukasz Prysiński, and Dariusz Wyspiański
University of Social Sciences, Łódź, Poland

Sylwia Przytuła
Wroclaw University of Economics; University of Social Sciences, Łódź, Poland

Czesław Sikorski
Department of Management, University of Łódź, Poland

Łukasz Sułkowski
Jagiellonian University, Poland

Dariusz Doliński and Tomasz Grzyb

Social Influence in Management – Possibilities for Using the "Power of WE" in the Everyday Work of a Manager

Preparation of this chapter was financially supported by grant BST/WROC/2017/A/02. *Correspondence concerning this chapter should be addressed to Dariusz Dolinski, SWPS University of Social Sciences and Humanities, Faculty of Psychology in Wroclaw, ul. Ostrowskiego 30B, 53-238 Wroclaw, Poland. E-mail: ddolinsk@swps.edu.pl.*

Abstract: This chapter depicts six rules of social influence, proposed by Robert Cialdini, and confirms they can be applied to different areas in management. It also analyses the seventh rule of influence, called "unity" or "Power of We" and proves its presence in organizations. The paper provides conditions that make it more likely for the rule to occur and clarifies the role of cultural impact in it.

Keywords: social influence, "Power of We", management, cultural context

Robert Cialdini proposed six universal rules of social influence that can be useful in various related fields, including in other-oriented activities of a manager. In his most recent book titled *Pre-suasion*, Cialdini elaborates his theoretical proposition with the addition of a seventh rule that he calls the "Power of WE." The authors of the present chapter present their considerations concerning the role of this particular rule in the activities of a manager, and they also give consideration to the role of the culture in which such activities are conducted. They conclude that paying heed to knowledge from the field of psychology can be very helpful in optimizing processes of people management, but the cultural context in which those actions are to be taken should always be given proper consideration.

With the 1985 publishing of his book *Influence. The Psychology of Persuasion*, Robert Cialdini – a professor at Arizona State University – became one of the most influential scholars not only in the field of psychology, but also in other areas of science (primarily marketing, sociology, and political science). It also rapidly turned out that the theoretical proposal he offers in that book can be of exceptional usefulness in the field of management. This book, which has been translated into dozens of languages and has sold over 3,000,000 copies worldwide, introduced a new and unusually catchy classification of social influence rules. While it was grounded firmly in science and built around a solid scientific methodology, it was written in exceptionally simple language. Cialdini succeeded in avoiding both scientific psychological jargon and trivialization of the issue presented. This led to the book achieving immediate popularity among practitioners-managers, individuals in charge of groups of people, or more generally anyone who deals with other people in their line of work. What is more, this book, despite the over three decades that have passed since it was published, remains the first piece of literature introducing psychology to these practitioners, and is continually reprinted and read (Cialdini, 2007).

In his book Cialdini advances the rather surprising hypothesis that the vast majority of the diverse techniques effective in influencing other people operate based on the activation of one of six fundamental psychological mechanisms (or combinations of those mechanisms) (see Fig.1). What is the strength and appeal of these "Six powers of influence?" It would seem that the primary answer is their intuitiveness and simplicity. Discussing each of the six rules in turn, Cialdini points out the scientific bases of their effectiveness, but also presents a range of examples, frequently anecdotal, of their practical application. We shall take a closer look at them, although we will not describe them in great detail, as interested readers can easily learn more from Cialdini's original book (if they have not done so already, which seems more than unlikely) or the numerous treatments of the issue already published. Our objective is rather to present a certain starting point for further considerations of the usefulness and universality of some of those rules (and their contemporary implications) in the daily work of a manager.

1 Reciprocity

This rule states that people strive for symmetry in interpersonal relations, and if they receive some good from another person, they feel obliged to reciprocate. Thus, if you wish to boost the chances that your request will be fulfilled (doing a task, achieving a goal) by a particular person, you should first do something for the benefit of that individual. For example, you should be considerate, or give them a small gift, etc. Such an action evokes in your interlocutor a feeling of obligation to return the consideration, and there is a greater chance they will do what you ask of them. This is precisely why people who receive a small piece of cheese to sample from a hostess then accede to her request to purchase a pound of that

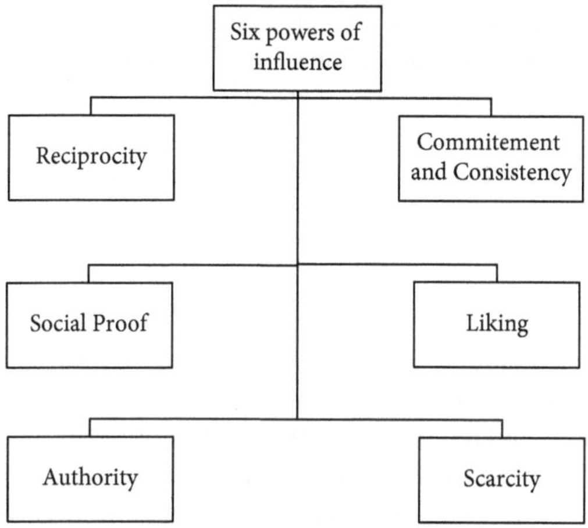

Fig. 1: Six powers of social influence.

same cheese, or an upset and irritated customer who encounters a pleasant salesperson also becomes pleasant and courteous.

2 Commitment and consistency

The next rule is based on the belief that people desire to be perceived as coherent and consistent, and also wish to view themselves in the same way. Thus, if you want to ask them to do something they may find difficult and bothersome, start with something easier that causes fewer problems. If people first agree to fill in a blank schedule of shifts for the upcoming week (which should not take more than fifteen minutes), it is more probable they will remain at work two hours later to complete this schedule. However, if you asked them at once to sacrifice their private time and plans already made, you should expect that in all likelihood they will refuse.

3 Social proof

We are, as social psychologist Eliott Aronson tells us in his classic formulation, social animals (Aronson, 2010). This means *inter alia* that our behaviours are heavily influenced by the people around us. As the English saying goes, "when in doubt, follow the crowd," and this is precisely the sense of the social proof rule. People (particularly in conditions of uncertainty) have a greater tendency to copy the behaviours of others in their surroundings than they do to maintain their own judgements and convictions. The information that some insurance company boasts the largest number of clients in Europe leads to that number of clients growing even more, and an advert claiming that the majority of people choose a certain pain relief medication should induce someone unsure of which pills they should take to just go along with the majority.

4 Liking

The idea that we are more eager to fulfil the request of someone we like than of someone we do not is more than trivial. Employees will be more eager to carry out the instructions and requests of managers they feel a greater affinity for. Less trivial, however, is that this can be achieved in various ways – through demonstrating closeness with employees, shared interests and experiences, spending time together, or building relationships that go beyond those based on the workplace hierarchy. One of the most important determinants of liking other people is the conclusion that we have something in common with them. An employee's observation that the boss also likes rock music or is a fan of the same basketball team is thus more significant than it may seem at first glance.

5 Authority

People tend to concur in their opinions, views, and actions with people they consider to be authorities. They will thus be likely to consider that a given means of solving a problem, performing a task, or achieving a goal is better if it is supported by the opinion of a person who enjoys the status of authority (a recognized specialist in a given field, a person with extensive experience, etc.). Such requests made by authorities are fulfilled more frequently than when they are advanced by "average Joes and Janes." The standard example of such obedience to commands made by authorities is the experiments conducted by Stanley Milgram (Milgram, 1974) and their later replications (Dolinski & Grzyb, 2016; Grzyb & Doliński, 2017). In these experiments, it was demonstrated that when commanded to by an authority (psychology professor), people are inclined to do things which they themselves believe to be wrong and harmful – in other words, to shock other participants with electricity as punishment for improperly performing a task. It should be added, however, that significant influence over others can be wielded not only by "real" authorities, but also by individuals who merely give the impression of being authorities (e.g., possessing some of the trappings of authority). This is why an actor advertising toothpaste on TV wears a white apron. There is no need to present the actor as a dentist (and thus an authority on issues of oral hygiene); it is sufficient that she looks like a dentist.

6 Scarcity

The attractiveness of a specific option or choice made is greater when the choice is one of greater difficulty. For example, employees are more motivated to participate in some company program if it is presented to them as exclusive and intended only for select members of the organization. The mechanism underlying the effectiveness of this rule is based, among other things, on the theory of reactance (Brehm, 1966), which indicates a link between the perceived attractiveness of a choice and a hindrance in making it, or even the threat that it will not be possible to make. Things which are rare or inaccessible also come across as particularly attractive to people. This is why some people are prepared to wait a year and a half for an exclusive model of a car, while others decide to purchase a house in a new estate only because the developer has announced that it is the last home left for sale.

The exceptionally synthetic rules described here rapidly became tools for managing people and teams of people. And yet since the time the first edition of Robert Cialdini's book was published we have seen many works demonstrating the application of social influence in management (np.: Aral & Walker, 2014; Gass & Seiter, 2015; Hambrick & Lovelace, 2018), Cialdini's offering continues to find takers. It forms the basis of both academic lectures in management and training workshops with a more practical orientation. What makes it so attractive? As we may suspect, it is first and foremost its simplicity and easy adaptation to concrete situations in organizations. Another important aspect seems to be its intuitiveness – let us observe that Cialdini provides managers with simple tools they can employ immediately. They do not require any deep changes in the design of one's own behaviour, nor particularly refined psychological knowledge (distinguishing them from, for example, the model offered by Petty & Cacioppo, 1986, or other complicated theoretical constructs). Cialdini's rules of influence are also – particularly important for international corporations – relatively divorced from cultural context, and thus can be applied without extensive modifications in all branches of transnational companies.

In analyzing the possibilities for applying rules of social influence in management, however, the issue of cultural differences cannot be entirely ignored. This has been demonstrated in a particularly interesting manner by Richard Nisbett (2004) in reference to assessment of the morality of employees and people applying for work; other scholars have also indicated the necessity of accounting for cultural differences in the use of various management tools (Chatterjee, Lubatkin, Schweiger, & Weber, 1992; Hall & Hall, 1989; Kawar, 2012). Robert Cialdini himself has also long taken into consideration cultural and intercultural aspects. The beginning of the century saw the publication of a collective monograph with the compelling title *The Practice of Social Influence in Multiple Cultures* (Wosinska, Cialdini, Barrett, & Reykowski, 2001), which I coedited. This book also includes a chapter on the strength of the impact of two social influence rules (commitment/consistency and social proof) in two different cultures (Cialdini, Wosinska, Barrett, Butner, & Gornik-Durose, 2001). Studies were conducted in the United States and Poland. It was assumed that while both rules would prove effective tools of social influence in both cultures, commitment/consistency would be more effective in the more individualistic of the two (i.e., in the USA), while social proof would be more effective in the more collectivist culture (i.e., in Poland). The results of the studies confirmed these assumptions. However, it also turned out that of greater importance than cultural norms were the individual norms espoused by individuals themselves. Thus, the commitment/consistency rule has a stronger influence on individualistic-oriented Poles than does social proof, while collectivist-oriented Americans are influenced to a greater extent by social proof than by commitment/consistency.

In his newest writings, Cialdini even more emphatically indicates elements of culture as significant predictors in decision-making with regards to specific tools. In his book *Pre-suasion* (Cialdini, 2016), he presents a range of behaviours and strategies which facilitate the application of social influence rules with significantly more attention to cultural specificity. Cialdini even suggests considering the application of something that, from a certain perspective, can be called a seventh rule of influence, termed "unity" or "Power of WE."

Studies demonstrating how the similarity to people making requests leads to considering those individuals and oneself in terms of the category "we," which in turn impacts the propensity to accede to their requests, have been known to social psychology for many years; however, it should be emphasized that – in the opinion of the authors of the present chapter – not to the extent they deserve. One example comes from studies by Jerry Burger and collaborators (Burger, Messian, Patel, del Prado, & Anderson, 2004) demonstrating how the discovery of "incidental similarities," with one asking for help, increased the chance that the request would be met with compliance. In this study, people who discovered (naturally, with the help of a clever experimental design) that they shared a surprising similarity with another participant (very similar fingerprints, which is exceptionally unusual) then became more inclined to comply with that individual's requests. Numerous examples of similar experiments are given by

Gass and Seiter (2015) in their review of studies devoted to the issue. However, the largest collection of publications demonstrating a link between treating someone as a member of one's "own" group and receptivity to social influence, as it occurs, belongs to Robert Cialdini.

In a series of studies (Goldstein, Cialdini, & Griskevicius, 2008), it was demonstrated that, for example, hotel guests were most strongly encouraged to reuse their hotel towels (which, as all hotel guests are aware, is at least officially intended to help support the natural environment, but incidentally helps the hotel owner save a few pennies) not when it was justified by contributions made by the hotel to environmental groups, but rather when the universality of such behaviours was cited. Characteristically, the argument was invoked that after a single use of a towel, the majority of guests at THAT hotel do not leave it on the floor. Interestingly, an even higher percentage of repeat towel usage was reported when guests were informed that previous guests staying IN THAT ROOM had exhibited such behaviour. People staying in the same hotel are to some degree "our folk," while those staying in the same room of the hotel are even more "our folk." Other studies (Griskevicius, Tybur, Sundie, Cialdini, & Miller, 2007) demonstrated the role played in shaping behaviours by social norms referring to people similar to ourselves. In a series of experiments (primarily concerning various types of pro-ecological behaviours) Cialdini showed people's eagerness to engage in activity protecting the natural environment when they are more convinced that such activity is the norm in their milieu. In other words, ecological justifications of such activities were of less importance than the fact that people similar to the study participants had performed those activities – "our folk." In a subsequent text (Cialdini et al., 2006) it was demonstrated how manipulation of social behavioural norms (again, referring mainly to one's "own group") can enhance the effectiveness of social influence. Interestingly, here the researchers showed that people are inclined to imitate others from their own group both when it comes to desirable and undesirable behaviours. A national park in Arizona had a problem with tourists taking pieces of petrified sequoias as souvenirs. Employees of the park thus put up signs with the alarming message that a great deal of tourists were devastating nature in that very manner. Contrary to their intentions, it turned out that occurrences of such pathological behaviour increased! Cialdini and his collaborators demonstrated that signs informing tourists that the vast majority of visitors to the park left it in precisely the condition they found it may be more effective. Let us observe that in the first case, the addressee of the message may interpret it thusly: "since other tourists - people like me - do it, there mustn't be anything wrong with it, so I can do it to," while in the second case: “since the norm is that tourists, and thus people like me, don’t take anything from the park, I should behave in the same way.” It is worth noting as an aside that, in reference to managerial practice, one may draw the conclusion that if we wish to combat inappropriate behaviours exhibited by some group of employees, a better strategy is to emphasize the prevalence of desirable behaviours rather than criticize frequent inappropriate and pathological ones. It can particularly be problematic when we emphasize that such actions are commonplace.

Returning to the main topic, let us observe that one aspect which remains unclear in the studies described above is that of the nature of the factor we may call “being own folk.” Is “own folk” a binary factor, or is it gradable – “a bit,” “a little more,” etc.? The same is applicable to people who are outside the group of “own folk” – from the perspective of social influence, are all of them equally alien, or is there a certain hierarchy, a gradation? In other words, are there people “more alien” and “less alien?” These are questions to which (we hope that only briefly) knowledge from the field of social influence processes does not offer clear answers.

All of the studies described above led Robert Cialdini to advance his hypothesis of the existence of a “seventh rule of social influence” he calls “The Power of WE.” At the same time, it would seem that this rule can be exceptionally useful when applied in business, particularly in the managerial context. Examples confirming this hypothesis can also be found in many organizations and companies. Let us cite one such case as an example. The Polish enterprise “Promotech,” based in Białystok, is engaged in the production of magnetic systems for industry (magnetic claws, crane elements, etc.). Like many other companies, it was hit hard by the decline in the European economy during the years 2008–2009. In spite of the fact that the company turned a profit in 2008 (just over EUR 1,000,000 on sales of roughly EUR 14,000,000), 2009 began with a clear and significant drop in orders. The company’s managers decided to initiate a round of wage cuts, consistent with the notion of workers’ solidarity. “We decided that just like we worked together during the good times, we should make it through the bad times together as well,” said Marek Siergiej, one of Promotech’s managers. As it turned out, a significant portion of the company’s staff (it should be emphasized, however, that not all of them) decided to accept a reduction in wages and employee benefits. As a result, while sales in 2009 dropped by 50 % to just over EUR 7,000,000, that year the company did not make a loss, but rather turned a profit (a modest one of EUR 500,000). Yet the mere fact of not making a loss in such a difficult period can be treated as a success in economic terms, while at the same time proves how important it is to foster the notion of “We” in respect to the entire organization.

Most likely, if this had not been accomplished, Promotech would not have survived at all.

Why does awareness of the effectiveness of this rule seem particularly important in managing people? As usual, there are several reasons. Of course, the most important is the creation of a sort of group identity for all members of the organization and enhancing the strength of employees' identification with the company. Employees become an integral part of the organization, with a deep awareness of their importance in the functioning of the entire structure.

It would seem that another rule of social influence described by Cialdini is (at least to a certain degree) involved: reciprocity. Employees who felt respected and valued, and who were aware that they were remunerated well during prosperous times, may have felt a duty of gratitude to the company itself and to accept reduced wages when tough times came. It should be observed here that reciprocity is a process drawn out over time. In accepting a temporary reduction in wages, lowered bonuses, cuts to social benefits, etc., during the hard times, not only is an employee giving back for the good things that came when the company was flush, but also has the right to count on a significant pay rise when prosperity returns. This, however, is only possible in conditions of significant interpersonal trust, which is in turn supported by thinking in terms of WE (we: all employees of the company) rather than US vs. THEM (us – employees, them – management and ownership).

Another factor allowing companies like Promotech to survive during a severe economic crisis is enhanced internal motivation to work. Employees aware that they constitute an important part of the organization can tell themselves "I'm not doing this only for myself – I'm responsible for the team, for my 'own folk." This is only possible when employees think in terms of the category of "we" being analyzed here, and thus feel like a member of a greater community. Concentration exclusively on one's own perspective and own interests (thinking exclusively in terms of "I") would require leaving as quickly as possible a workplace that had stopped paying high wages.

Using the technique "Power of WE" thus constitutes outstanding preparation for "tough times" – temporary drops in sales, global economic difficulties, currency fluctuations, the threat of inflation, or recession. Employees with a deep-rooted awareness of belonging to an organization can help it manage better in the face of deteriorating external circumstances. Employees who do not feel this bond can add additional fuel to the fire when the organization is in crisis.

Of course, dynamic intra-group phenomena are exceptionally important in this process. Employees who see that their co-workers identify with the company, and in spite of the tough times remain in their posts, agreeing to reductions in their salaries, are inclined to do the same. Of course, if they saw that their co-workers rejected this course and decided to go on strike or to seek employment elsewhere, they would in all likelihood behave in the same manner. In turn, we may observe here the unusual role played by another rule that Cialdini discusses: the rule of authority. This does not necessarily mean epistemic authority (the perception of someone as an expert and specialist in a given area), but rather social authority. A charismatic employee about whom nobody thinks will remain with the company in times of crisis merely to protect her own particular interests can by her own example galvanize many other employees. This process can take on a very interesting dynamic. When a change of opinions begins among some people within a given group, they can, in certain conditions, very quickly and effectively attract others to their side. What are these conditions?

One of the most important theories referring to such dynamic situations is the conception advanced by Serge Moscovici (1976, 1985; Moscovici, Mucchi-Faina, and Maas, 1994) detailing the conditions in which a minority can influence the majority to such a degree that it starts becoming the majority itself. As a range of empirical studies has demonstrated, the influence of a minority on the majority is particularly likely in a situation where the minority is, on one hand, consistent in the presentation of its views, while on the other hand coherent, *id est* when particular members of a particular minority demonstrate exactly the same attitude. It would seem that this situation leads to prominence of so-called informational social influence. Members of the majority, seeing that other people are consistent in giving voice to an alternative view and refuse to submit to the opinion of the majority, may arrive at the conclusion that the minority is correct. These circumstances lead to people in the majority engaging in reflection, asking themselves what arguments the minority has. Familiarizing themselves with these arguments and confronting them with their own views can lead to a change in attitudes and opinions among the majority group.

Of course additional conditions must also be met for this to occur. Among those conditions, Moskovici assigns a particular role to the open conflict of views of the minority and the majority, as well as the attendant interaction among members of those groups. Also of importance is that the view of the minority is stated loudly and explicitly, which leads the members of the majority group to conclude that representatives of the minority will not hesitate to publicly defend their position. If they do so essentially in spite of the majority, they must be very convinced as to their correctness. Thus, their arguments are deserving of serious attention. At the same time, however, in disputes with representatives of the majority, representatives of the minority should accept their arguments and views in reference to other issues. This indicates that the minority cannot be accused of cognitive rigidity, dogmatism, and blind obstinacy. This all facilitates a change of views among the members of the majority group – they see that on one hand the minority is certain of the correctness of their views, while on the other hand they are prepared to engage in discussion and are open to their opponents' arguments. In addition, yet another phenomenon can be perceived in the phenomenon under discussion: based on the conflict of the minority with the majority, the exchange of views, and the unshaken certainty of the minority, some of the people who declare merely formal allegiance to the majority group but in fact in hold different views can conclude that there are others who think similarly to them. In such a situation, it is easier for them to declare what had previously been hidden beliefs and convictions.

It should be noted as an aside that it is the influence of the minority on the majority (and not of the majority on the minority) which forms the foundations of development and progress. New ideas born in the minds of individuals rarely concern issues on which people in general have no opinion. Quite the opposite: these ideas are frequently in total opposition to that which has been "settled" for ages. After all, people were once entirely certain that the Earth is flat and located at the centre of the universe. The consistent repetition by an individual at first, then by a small group of people, and ultimately by a very numerous collection of individuals that this is not, in fact, the case, led to the majority today being firmly convinced that the Earth is shaped like a ball and orbits around the Sun. If it were impossible for the minority to influence the majority, humanity would never accept this new (and previously not at all obvious) idea.

It would seem that the most significant changes in organization also consist not in the majority exerting pressure on a minority that finally falls into line, but rather in a minority successfully convincing the majority to its vision. This can concern both issues directly related to a company's operations (such as the mode of production of certain goods or provision of services, marketing strategy, pricing policy) and solutions related to motivating employees, internal communication, or organization of the workday.

Returning in this context to Robert Cialdini's conception of "Power of WE," it should be observed that the impact of the minority on the majority will be easier in conditions where both the minority and the majority are perceived not in categories of "us versus them" ("us" – people with certain views versus "them" – people with different views), but only in terms of "we" (e.g., "we" – employees of the same company). In these conditions it is easier to listen carefully to the arguments of those with other points of view, and to accept those arguments if they turn out to be sensible (Crano, 2018). By the same token, the conception of Serge Moscovici intersects with Cialdini's "Power of WE": each of them adds detail, complements, and enriches the other.

In summary, it is worth pointing out that Cialdini's proposition remains relatively fresh, and it is even difficult to classify definitively. It may turn out (at least, it cannot be entirely excluded) that referring to it as the "seventh rule of social influence" is a bit of an overstatement. Perhaps it should be treated rather as an amplifier, a certain factor modifying the impact of the remaining rules (for example, commitment and consistency can have a much stronger impact when the object towards which we feel obliged to engage is someone we can describe as a member of our own group, "our folk"). It should be kept in mind, however, that from the perspective of its practical application this does not change much – it remains just as useful. And managers capable of convincing members of their teams that they belong to one and the same group (which also entails taking responsibility and engaging in work oriented on the common good) will simply be more effective managers.

In this context, we are also faced with the question of culture's impact on the strength of the impact exhibited by the "Power of WE" rule. It would seem natural that it should be greater in countries where membership in a given community is of particular importance for the identity of individuals (and thus in cultures where social identity is more important than individual identity). It should therefore play a particular role in the societies of the Far East and Latin America. On the other hand, things might not be so simple. Indeed, we should point out a certain paradox: in individualistic cultures (e.g., the United States, Great Britain) team sports (basketball, hockey, baseball, football) are more popular than individual ones. In the collectivist countries of the East (e.g., China, Japan), individual sports enjoy exceptional popularity (e.g., judo, table tennis, badminton, sumo wrestling). Perhaps it is the case that the experience of community in particular situations can be of more importance to people from individualistic cultures (for whom such an experience is rare) than for people from collectivist cultures (for which that experience is commonplace).

The idea of "Power of WE" is too new for there to be any empirical studies that would provide a direct answer to that question. We therefore do not know whether this tool of social influence would be more effective in the hands of managers from the West or the East. That said, we do not doubt that even those cultures where its effectiveness would be reduced, this would only be a relative reduction. People from diverse cultures are characterized by more similarities than differences. The need for belonging to a group, the need to think of themselves and other people in terms of "we" can be present to differing degrees across human communities, but it is universal and omnipresent. For this reason, we too are deeply convinced that the use of this social influence tool must be beneficial to managers around the world.

References

Aral, S., & Walker, D. (2014). Tie strength, embeddedness, and social influence: A large-scale networked experiment. *Management Science, 60*(6), 1352–1370.

Aronson, E. (2010). *Not by chance alone: My life as a social psychologist*. Basic Books.

Brehm, J. W. (1966). *A theory of psychological reactance*. Oxford, England: Academic Press.

Burger, J. M., Messian, N., Patel, S., del Prado, A., & Anderson, C. (2004). What a coincidence! The effects of incidental similarity on compliance. *Personality and Social Psychology Bulletin, 30*(1), 35–43.

Chatterjee, S., Lubatkin, M. H., Schweiger, D. M., & Weber, Y. (1992). Cultural differences and shareholder value in related mergers: Linking equity and human capital. *Strategic Management Journal, 13*(5), 319–334.

Cialdini, R. (2016). *Pre-Suasion: A revolutionary way to influence and persuade*. Simon and Schuster.

Cialdini, R. B. (2007). *Influence: The psychology of persuasion*. Collins: New York.

Cialdini, R. B., Demaine, L. J., Sagarin, B. J., Barrett, D. W., Rhoads, K., & Winter, P. L. (2006). Managing social norms for persuasive impact. *Social Influence, 1*(1), 3–15.

Cialdini, R. B., Wosinska, W., Barrett, D. W., Butner, J., Gornik-Durose, M. (2001). The differential impact of two social influence principles on individualists and collectivists in Poland and the United States. In W. Wosinska, R. B. Cialdini, D. W. Barrett, J. Reykowski (Eds.). Applied social research. The practice of social influence in multiple cultures. (pp. 33–50). Mahwah, NJ, US: Lawrence Erlbaum Associates Publishers.

Dolinski, D., & Grzyb, T. (2016). One serious shock versus gradated series of shocks: Does "multiple feet-in-the-door" explain obedience in Milgram studies?. *Basic and Applied Social Psychology, 38*(5), 276–283.

Gass, R. H., & Seiter, J. S. (2015). *Persuasion: Social influence and compliance gaining*. Routledge.

Goldstein, N. J., Cialdini, R. B., & Griskevicius, V. (2008). A room with a viewpoint: Using social norms to motivate environmental conservation in hotels. *Journal of Consumer Research, 35*(3), 472–482.

Griskevicius, V., Tybur, J. M., Sundie, J. M., Cialdini, R. B., & Miller, G. F., & Kenrick, D. T. (2007). Blatant benevolence and conspicuous consumption:

When romantic motives elicit strategic costly signals. *Journal of Personality and Social Psychology*, 93, 85–102.

Grzyb, T., & Doliński, D. (2017). Perpetrator as a potential victim. Does threatened retaliation from the victim reduce obedience towards authority?. *Psychologica Belgica*, *57*(2), 123–132.

Hall, E. T., & Hall, M. R. (1989). *Understanding cultural differences*. Intercultural press.

Hambrick, D. C., & Lovelace, J. B. (2018). The role of executive symbolism in advancing new strategic themes in organizations: A social influence perspective. *Academy of Management Review*, *43*(1), 110–131.

Kawar, T. I. (2012). Cross-cultural differences in management. *International Journal of Business and Social Science*, *3*(6), 105–112.

Milgram, S. (1974). *Obedience to authority. An experimental view*. Harper: New York.

Nisbett, R. (2004). *The geography of thought: How Asians and Westerners think differently... and why*. Simon and Schuster.

Petty, R. E., & Cacioppo, J. T. (1986). Message elaboration versus peripheral cues. *Communication and persuasion* (141–172). New York: Springer.

Wosinska, W., Cialdini, R.B., Barrett, D.W., & Reykowski, J. (2009) (Eds.) *The practice of social influence in multiple cultures*. Erlbaum: Mahwah and London.

Czesław Sikorski

Leaderless Organization or Organization of Leaders

Abstract: Giving the explanation what authoritarianism really is, as well as describing all the determinants of relations between a superior and his/her subordinates within such system, the paper also presents its drawbacks and methods of manipulation. Moreover, it shows why the departure from authoritarian leadership is necessary and highlights the directions of change. It presents new types of leadership and future form of the organizational power relation.

Keywords: authoritarianism, stereotypes, leadership, information revolution and globalization impact

1 Authoritarian power

Authoritarianism is a form of power relations in which we deal with the unidirectional influence of the superior on the subordinates. It is an asymmetric relationship, characterized by a substantially different superior position relative to the position of subordinates. The former has the exclusive right to influence subordinate persons, to set their goals, to assign tasks, to shape their behaviour and way of thinking. The subordinates are obliged to adapt to the will and expectations of the superior. Activity and creativity are attributed to the superior; the subordinates are to be passive and obedient. This way of exercising power – and its modes of interaction between superior and subordinates, such as dialogue or negotiation – is the opposite of democracy. In authoritarianism, dictatorship and manipulation are ways of executing power relations.

The need for authoritarian power is usually explained by the uniqueness of the mind and character of the superior, usually referred to as the leader or even the ruler or chief. It is the genius of the leader who sees further and broader than the others, that makes subordinates, also sometimes called proponents or even followers, submit themselves to him. In the culture of power, which is at the root of authoritarianism, there is no need to justify authoritarian relationships. In the simplistic view it is assumed that all authority should be of such character – the superior is to think and make decisions, and the subordinate is to execute the superior's commands. This view refers to the oldest traditions of power. Obedience to the superior was justified through the power of God. Of course, not every leader could aspire to the role of God's governor, as this was reserved for kings and emperors, but every ruler represented some of God's gifts.

This view on the mysterious element, which justifies the absolute dominance of certain people over others, is seen in many conservative social concepts as a guarantee of law and order. The conservative view on the need for a stable social hierarchy can be found in the writings of politicians and moralists from the early stages of capitalism. Inequality in positions and social roles, advocated by conservatives, once led Hobbes to distinguish between two types of people: those who place prestige above security, and those who place security over the risk associated with the pursuit of prestige – namely: the masters and the slaves.[1] In old literature a characteristic pair of figures quite monotonously appeared: a lord and a servant. The former tried to conquer the world; the latter regarded himself most fortunate when he could faithfully serve his master.

Authoritarianism, as we can see, is not solely a feature of the leader, but it is characteristic for both sides of the power relationship. Only then does it find an actual reflection in the thinking and behaviour of the people, and leads to the consequences considered by proponents of this form of power to be desirable. In order for authoritarianism to occur in its purist form the need for domination of the superior must meet the need of the subordinate to submit himself. In other words: if someone wants to rule, they must find those who want to be ruled, which is usually not difficult. Many people easily give up their independence by looking for role models to whom they are ready to surrender completely. Authoritarian submission lies in the recognition of the superior's vision as their own, and acceptance of the assumption that his rationality frees his subordinates from the duty of independent thinking. Hence it is only a step from regarding a supervisor as a genius, who, thinking for his subordinates, relieves them of this abominable duty. Here too one can notice the influence of the old myth, whose various versions appear especially in difficult and crisis situations when people doubt their own strengths. This is the myth of the messiah, the redeemer, the guide, the providential man who will come and tell them what to do, who will take care of them and lead them along the right path. Such a saviour must be trusted completely and uncritically. He must inspire in his followers' zealous subordination, no matter what ideas he has and what he does. His every decision is the confirmation of his genius. And people often do just that. Their unshaken faith in the wisdom of their leader cannot be undermined even by his most stupid and absurd actions. The leader appears as his followers want to see him.

1 Quot. after: P. Manent, *Intelektualna historia liberalizmu*, Arcana, Kraków 1994, p. 67.

The conviction of the helplessness of ordinary people, which can be handled by a few great leaders, has been paving the way for authoritarian cultural patterns since time immemorial. Authoritarianism would have never been applied in practice if the need for it had been possessed exclusively by people of power. Authoritarianism works thanks to ordinary people, subordinates who want to have a leader and guardian. Referring to the absolute power exercised by an authoritarian individual, Hobbes rejects its religious interpretation: the ruler does not represent divine power, but the weakness of his subjects – for they have endowed him with absolute power to remedy their own weakness.[2] A similar phenomenon in the animal world is indicated by T.E. Rowell in his study on baboons. He states that the hierarchy is the result of the behaviour of the subordinate individuals, and therefore is imposed by the animals placed in its lowest, not the highest rank.[3]

The essence of authoritarianism is not only the asymmetry in the position of superior and subordinates, but the asymmetry of mutual expectations of both parties of power relations. These expectations are opposed but at the same time complementary. The superior expects obedience from subordinates and subordinates expect the superior's care. One supports the other: the more subordinates obey the superior, the more care they can expect from him, and vice versa: the greater care the superior takes of his subordinates, the more they obey his will.

What does care and obedience mean in this case? Care means protection against a variety of threats. Subordinates, experiencing care from their superior, feel exempted from the obligation to guard their own affairs and from the responsibility for them. There is someone, incomparably stronger and wiser than them, who will take care of it. So they can stop worrying about something they do not know or are not familiar with and attend to much more pleasant things instead. The stronger the subordinates experience the care of the superior, the more they fix their own immaturity, i.e. the reluctance to bear personal responsibility for what happens to them. The subordinates become passive, completely dependent on their superior, convinced of the external location of the control over their actions. But just then, the supervisor can most easily enforce the obedience of subordinates. Since subordinates feel completely dependent on him, they must fully submit to him. Obedience means in this case the readiness to

2 Ibidem, pp. 51–52.

3 Quot. after: E. Fromm, *Anatomia ludzkiej destrukcyjności*, Dom Wydawniczy Rebis, Poznań 2002, p. 132.

accurately fulfil the orders of the superior without any attempt to critically evaluate and discuss them.

In authoritarian power, the subordinates treat the superior as a leader who knows best what to do and how. Opposition to him would be not only foolish, but above all it would deprive them of their sense of confidence and security, which they care most about. In turn the superior treats the subordinates as tools that he must use to achieve his goals. And a tool is good when it obeys the will of its user, that is, it does not cause trouble in service. The authoritarian superior does not like when subordinates ask unnecessary questions or, worse yet, offer solutions alternative to the ones he has accepted. Subordinates should be obedient, not active. Thinking is left to the boss.

What kind of people are the subordinates who assign such roles to their superiors, and what kind of people are the superiors who take such roles? In short – they are each other's opposite. So subordinates have a strong external sense of control that makes them see the leader as their guardian and expert, while the leader has a strong internal sense of control that triggers in him the need for self-fulfilment through the authority, and in the person of the subordinate he seeks a tool to accomplish his goals. The subordinate has low self-esteem, is susceptible to influences and in the person of the leader he wants to see his idol, whereas the leader is self-confident, wants to influence others and impose his own order and in the subordinate he sees his follower. In the authoritarian power relation, one more kind of asymmetry is worth pointing out. The great confidence, shown by subordinates towards the leaders, clashes with the distrust on the part of the leader shown towards the subordinates. This is evident in many authoritarian cultures. The results show that Chinese managers are not accustomed to showing confidence to their subordinates as they are convinced that this would undermine their authority among people with lower social status.[4]

Different, but also complementary, in authoritarian power are the means with which the superior and the subordinates try to enforce their expectations. The superior can use for this purpose two well-known methods, namely, the ability to induce anxiety and the ability to seduce. These skills can be used to distinguish two types of authoritarian leaders, though there are also superiors who master both of these skills and use them interchangeably.

The ability to induce anxiety is characteristic for tyrants, and involves demonstrating ruthlessness in applying penalties, the consequence of fulfilling the

4 K.Y. Wang, S. Clegg, *Trust and Decision Making: Are Managers Different in the People's Republic of China and in Australia?*, "Cross Cultural Management", No. 1, 2002.

threats and the annoyance of their effects on subordinates. This is due to the conviction that the secret of effective power lies in the effectiveness of convincing the subordinates of the inevitability of punishment for a lack of obedience, and of its painful consequences. In order for this type of authoritarian rule to meet the expectations of subordinates, they must be convinced that their leader is not only severe, but above all fair and occasionally also gracious. If that were not the case, if the superior were never successfully persuaded to resign from punishment, if in addition his behaviour were chimerical and unpredictable and his decisions were often unfair, then the superior not only would not reduce the sense of uncertainty in his subordinates but would also be an additional factor increasing this uncertainty. The authoritarian power would then lose its cultural basis ensuring its effectiveness, as it would no longer be liked by the subordinates. To such a model of a leader – stern but just and because of this predictable – many past rulers aspired. This model is often encountered even today. An example might be the style presented by Russian president Vladimir Putin, who occasionally performs spectacular actions, personally solving an array of problems in various places and punishing those officials who are not aware of human affairs or are ineffective. The president counts on the traditions of authoritarian rule in Russia, where people would like to trust a righteous and powerful tsar who can deal with the boyars that harm the people.

The ability to seduce is in turn typical of charismatic leaders who easily create and enforce their authority on subordinates. The authoritarian superior influences, in this case, the positive emotions of subordinates who respect him and obey him not because they fear him, but because they admire him and sometimes even love him. It is generally agreed that charisma manifests itself in the ability to articulate a vision that the subordinates are willing to consider as their own, not so much because of its rational justification, but by appealing to values that are important to them, attractive and unequivocal. It is crucial, therefore, to use appropriate language and appeal to the imagination. The ability to associate visions with historical events that relate to pride or to use current issues and events to spark ambition is particularly important in this case. The effectiveness of the charismatic leader greatly improves the more the values he invokes help his subordinates to have a clear picture of difficult situations. The ability to appeal to people and to find that tender thread is therefore a feature of a charismatic leader. The subordinates attribute extraordinary skills to their leader, which prompts them to unconditionally accept his authority. A charismatic leader may demand from his subordinates activity and initiative, and may not want to exercise authoritarian power. Unfortunately, as long as the basis of his authority is the subordinates' emotions, he cannot count on anything but the blind trust and enthusiastic realization of his commands. A charismatic leader must be an authoritarian leader even if he does not want to be. A leader of this type does not inspire subordinates; he seduces them, and thus restricts them. The more dominant, strong and creative the leader is, the weaker and less independent become his subordinates.

Regardless of whether ruled by a tyrant or a charismatic leader, subordinates have only one way to enforce the care of their superior. This method is the complete opposite of the ways of enforcing obedience. While the latter rely on the demonstration of any force, the enforcement of care consists of the consistent demonstration of weakness. The subordinates try to reassure their superior that they will not be able to cope without his help. Hence – continuous requests for interventions, play-safe behaviour, avoiding all risks or waiting for the supervisor's decision in even the simplest of cases. The weaker the subordinates feel, the greater the sense of power their superiors have. In authoritarian power, strength and weakness are mutually supportive and complementary. An authoritarian leader, irrespective of whether his authority is based on fear or love, is frightfully lonely. He is forbidden to share with his subordinates his doubts and fears. So the authoritarian leader is in a way a hostage of his subordinates: he must unceasingly play his role and embody what subordinates want to see in him.

2 Criticism of authoritarian power

2.1 The ethical aspect of authoritarianism

The criticism of authoritarianism results, among other things, from the moral assessment of the effects of such social relationships in which people, while abandoning their individuality, simultaneously resign from a part of their humanity. And a situation in which a good and wise leader carries out noble goals can be no justification. The only justification of leadership acceptable from a moral standpoint is the desire to empower subordinates, to develop and exploit their potential. In literature there are numerous warnings, and in practice – examples of the dangers associated with authoritarian leadership. D. McClelland warns against "power hungry" people, whose behaviour resembles the behaviour of people addicted to alcohol, drugs or gambling, and who are similarly aggressive and selfish.[5]

N.L. Ury, J. Brett and S.B. Goldberg have drawn attention to three basic ways of resolving disputes: by reconciling conflicting interests, by determining which

5 D. McClelland, *The Two Faces of Power*, "Journal of International Affairs", No. 1, 1970.

side is right and by showing who is stronger.[6] In the culture of authoritarianism the first two ways are rejected – a strong leader does not need to justify his decisions, does not have to explain anything, and in any case cannot give in to anyone. Even the slightest concession would be a sign of weakness, and therefore undermine the authority of the leader. Aggression is an intrinsic part of the culture of authoritarianism.

Permission for authoritarian aggression can be seen in tribute paid to the organizational autocrats, whose actions grow into legends and often serve as a model for effective leadership. For example, R. O'Brien, with visible admiration, describes the typical autocratic style of leadership behaviour of J.W. Marriott when he was still the owner of a small restaurant in Washington: "His managers had never known what time of day or night he would burst into the kitchen or the dining room and start checking the cleanliness in the refrigerator or the pantry, the freshness of the waiter's shirts, the dust on the pictures or chandeliers or under the table, or the shine of beer glasses. They knew perfectly well that if everything were not shining and gleaming, were not clean and perfect, they would have hell on earth."[7] One truly must have very little confidence in people to admire such a style of management, to confuse hysteria and rudeness with professionalism, and pettiness with perfectionism.

The aggression of an authoritarian leader does not always have to manifest itself in open coercion and discrimination against disobedient subordinates. Sometimes coercion is camouflaged, which is characteristic especially for leaders who have the ability to seduce their subordinates. Aggression in their rendition often involves the use of various forms of manipulation. These forms include, for example, provocation, which consists of forcing someone to behave in a manner that someone would like to avoid, and which is for him for some reason disadvantageous. A common way of provocation can be to annoy and tease the opponent, forcing him to be too emotional, extreme and therefore easily ridiculed and criticized. Provocation may also consist of attributing to the opponent the views that he does not actually represent.

Another form of manipulation is an intrigue that involves using other people's actions, unaware of the real purpose of the schemer. A leader who uses intrigue assigns the subordinates their roles in advance, and then, using his abilities to

---

6 N.L. Ury, J.M. Brett, S.B. Goldberg, *Getting Disputes Resolved*, Jossey-Bass, San Francisco 1988, p. 15.

7 Quot. after: F.G. Harmon, G. Jacobs, *The Vital Difference. Unleashing the Powers of Sustained Corporate Success*, http://mirainternational.com/books/difference/CHAP01.htm.

influence them, tries to get them to act, unconsciously playing these roles according to his script. The most effective in intrigue are the situations in which people come together in conflicts on the grounds of jealousy, a sense of injustice, the desire for revenge and so on.

Some of the authoritarian leaders' favourite methods of manipulation include infiltration, which involves introducing into the social group new members that affect the behaviour of people in the group as expected by the superior. They do this consciously, following the boss's instructions and expecting a reward in return. This interaction generally consists of presenting views or actions less popular in this group but at the same time concerning important issues, which causes ferment and promotes polarization.

The tendency to manipulate means the attachment of the superior to paternalism, which is an important component of the authoritarian attitude. Paternalism consists of treating subordinates like children in need of caring, which justifies the right to interfere in their personal affairs and the use of manipulation to achieve educational goals. The master of manipulation, Niccolo Machiavelli, not coincidentally, is treated as a model to follow by many leaders with such tendencies. Moreover, these leaders not only have no sense of moral misconduct, but on the contrary, they regard their conduct as a manifestation of moral responsibility for their subordinates, similar to that of parents responsible for their underage children.

2.2 Authoritarian stereotypes in the organization

The concepts of organizational power have undergone significant evolution in the twentieth century from authoritarianism to the participation of subordinates in management. Trends in the democratization of organizational power have been particularly strengthened and accelerated as a result of the information and education revolution. The former challenged the informational monopoly of a narrow group of managers, which was the basis for decision making, while the latter provided the broad range of employees with the ability to solve problems independently, thus far reserved for executives. However, the viability of authoritarian cultural stereotypes is large, and manifests itself even in the common definition, according to which the power consists of achieving the manager's goals with the hands of his subordinates. Although in this definition the objective attitude towards the subordinates is too visible, it is often quoted in modern management textbooks.

In management practice, the traces of attachment to the authoritarian power conception are most often expressed in relation to the career model, the centralization of decision-making powers and communication with subordinates. It is hard to resist the conviction that the vitality of these stereotypes results not so much from their questionable usability in the era of information civilization, as above all from the difficulty of becoming independent of the narcotic of power in its classic sense.

Vertical career stereotype

The strength of this stereotype lies in this that the word "promotion" is clearly associated with an upward shift in the hierarchy of power. Promoted is one who leads a larger team of people, larger or more powerful organizations or has gained a greater possibility to exert influence on people than ever before. Achievements in other fields outside of power may be called success, but if they do not entail an increase in power in any sense, they are rarely referred to as promotion. It seems that there is only one type of hierarchy in the common awareness – the hierarchy of power. Other hierarchies, which reflect the differences between people in different categories of achievement, are neither very expressive nor highly valued. The reason for this is the firmly held belief that these differences between people in various fields of activity eventually end up in the position occupied in the hierarchy of power. An old, well-known principle was that the manager should always be the best professional in the team. This principle seems to be common sense, because who is supposed to lead the team if not the one who knows the work best and knows how to do it best. So, success in the professional field is most often translated into promotion in the hierarchy of power in the organization. Such a promotion was also until recently a professional career determinant. Apart from artistic, scientific and sports activities which involved a relatively small proportion of society, the career meant the process of advancing to the next level in the hierarchy of power. It did not matter what someone has accomplished as a doctor, economist, engineer or lawyer; of utmost importance was which managerial position he got during his professional career. The more important director, president or chairman he was, the greater in a common sense career he made.

However, the conditions for the functioning of economic organizations in the era of information civilization cause that, in the interest of streamlining the information and decision-making processes, the intermediary management levels are eliminated in the organizational structure, leading to the flattening of the structure. The ladder of the hierarchy is becoming shorter, so the possibilities for vertical advancement are getting smaller and smaller. Another consequence of adapting the organization to the conditions of the contemporary market is the creation of temporary project teams, whose goal is a comprehensive execution of a complex task. These teams supplant the fixed industrial assemblies that were common in the era of industrial civilization, and which brought together specialists from one field to perform one repetitive function.

These circumstances make managerial advancement less and less attractive for at least two reasons: firstly, because the promotion ladder was shortened due to the drastic decrease in the number of managerial posts; secondly, because the power in the organization became unstable and transitive. The experience gained from working in project teams teaches that not only is the team temporary, but the manager is as well. When the task is done, probably someone else and probably only briefly will take control of the new team. This is a modern approach, called a process approach, which involves adjusting the team to the best possible task execution and not, as before, adapting the performance to the current capabilities of the team. Under these conditions, power loses the value of mystery and uniqueness, and becomes something common as a result of the casual division of organizational roles, depending on the type of task and the conditions of its implementation.

From this point of view, the well-established belief that a manager should be the best in the team, the one who knows best about the work to be done, cannot stand the criticism. It was customary to regard this conviction as a truism, without taking into account firstly its practical consequences in hierarchical structures, and, secondly, changes in the way tasks are performed in modern structures, especially networks. Bestowing managerial functions on outstanding specialists in traditional structures resulted, for the organization, in the limitation and sometimes even a total loss of the possibility to benefit from their professional skills. A talented designer became the project manager at the project office and was only partly able to devote himself to designing, and when he was promoted to the post of director of the office in recognition of his professional values, he then ceased to pursue his profession by devoting himself exclusively to management. In this way, the organizations lost good performers, often gaining poor managers in return.

The change in the way tasks are performed in many of today's organizations is based on the fact that professional expertise is needed in executive positions. Employed in these positions, professionals are autonomous in choosing the way of doing the work for which they are responsible. The managers, most often temporary, need to be able to coordinate their work effectively, and to do so the knowledge of the organization's priorities and the ability to analyze the components of the organizational environment are needed, more so than knowledge and professional skills with regard to the subject matter of their subordinates' work.

"Manager - the best professional" is a cultural myth established in times when work in teams was relatively simple and professionally homogeneous, which made it impossible to imagine another, beyond the managerial, career model.

In modern conditions, professional values – and not the value of power – are at the forefront. The sense of success and career achievement should be credited to those who are assigned increasingly more responsibilities, even if they were completely unrelated to performing managerial functions. The ability to perform these tasks should determine the employee's professional position and the social prestige associated with it. In today's organizations, which A.K. Koźmiński defines as being "enterprising," completely different employees are needed than in "commanding" organizations. Working in temporary task forces favours popularizing a professional rather than a managerial career model. Vertical advancement begins to be replaced by a horizontal promotion consisting of moving the employee to increasingly more difficult and more ambitious tasks, participating in increasingly elite teams, the so-called centres of excellence. Horizontal promotion means not only increasing prestige and financial gratification but, above all, improving the employee's brand in the labour market and in the working environment, effectively increasing his "market value." Underestimating a professional career and treating it as inferior to a managerial career indicates that there is no adaptation to the conditions of the information-civilization era, and may, in some employees, cause frustration and the lack of ability to fulfil their own potential.

Myth of centralization

The conviction that centralization of power increases control and allows for better governance of the state or management of the organization so often turned out to be false that its vitality is puzzling. Probably one of the reasons for this vitality is the old myth of a benevolent dictator who wants to do his best for his subjects, but his actions are interfered with by his inept or greedy intendants. The latter, through their powers, deform the ruler's intentions, and at the same time block or distort information about the actual state of affairs. They need to be deprived of these powers in order to make the good ruler have a direct influence on the course of affairs. For centuries many rulers, wishing to be considered "good," were eager to use the alibi of excessive distribution of their powers and their own limited abilities to exercise control. Today, nothing has changed in this regard. The statist tendencies in governing of the state appear frequently, especially as the centralization of power is of interest not only to those who exercise it, but also to the very citizens who do not have confidence in local authority for various reasons. The dream of "finally getting someone up at the top to deal with them" naturally makes people see hope in the headquarters.

The second cause of centralizing tendencies is due to the very nature of power. Montesquieu points it out in his famous observation: "An age-old experience teaches that any man who has power is inclined to abuse it."[8] The pursuit of greater power is a natural need for authoritarian leaders. This is often supported by the attitude of the subordinates themselves, who in the authoritarian relations of power willingly dispose of the remnants of independence and personal responsibility. Where getting rid of decision-making powers is out of the question for a variety of reasons, an authoritarian attitude can be recognized in play-safe behaviour so that the decision does not put the decision-maker at risk. As it has already been pointed out, under the authoritarianism, superiors have no confidence in their subordinates. In these conditions, it is difficult to expect an initiative from the subordinate and the undertaking of bold, innovative ways to solve problems. As it is well known, the level of trust in social relations in Poland is the lowest in Europe. Therefore, attitudes toward in organizations are not surprising. When deciding on tenders, for example, the company that offers the lowest price for the commissioned project usually wins, even if it is known in advance that the quality of the work will be terrible, and cooperation with this company will mean an array of troubles. But in Poland it cannot be otherwise, because what would the superiors or public opinion say, if the tender was won by the company with a higher bid than its competitors? The accusation of mismanagement and suspicion of corruption would be inevitable. Authoritarian distrust either favours centralization of power, or deforms decentralization and makes it fiction.

The concentration of decision-making powers at the highest levels of government can foster efficient implementation of organizational goals only for small organizations operating in a stable environment and performing simple tasks. In the event of failure to meet either of these conditions, the centralization of power leads to overloading decision-makers and over-concentration on managing current operations at the expense of long-term issues. To prevent this, the spread of management decreases, creating new managerial positions and levels of management, thus expanding the organizational hierarchy. This, in turn, makes the decision-making process time-consuming. The strongly fragmented hierarchical structure of the organization results in the dominance of vertical

8 Montesquieu, *O duchu praw*, chapter XI, KiW, Warszawa 1957, p. 4.

communication, oriented on the needs of power, but weakens the horizontal communication, oriented on the implementation of tasks.

The fact that in modern, horizontal organizational structures cultural myths about strengthening control by centralizing decisions is completely false, many authors argue. T. Peters writes on this point directly that the manager has real control today only when he can trust "thousands of unknown to him people who take the initiative, regardless of formal scopes of activities, who better serve clients, improve their work and work faster and flawlessly."[9]

It is also true that in hierarchical structures, shifting of decision-making powers and associated responsibility to higher levels of management serves not to reinforce but to weaken control. In Polish literature, Stanisław Kowalewski pointed it out long ago, arguing that the centralization of decisions undermines control because a manager at a higher level of management is not able to know the details of the case in which he decides. He must therefore base his decision on the suggestions of those who know the case better. This situation is much more convenient to committing abuse and manipulating subordinates than when the issues were resolved at a lower position where there is enough information to make a decision.[10]

According to Herbert Simon's definition of *lapidary*, decisions should be made where they can be made with the greatest competence.[11] And competence is determined by knowledge and access to information. Ordinary employees, by their very nature, have the quickest access to relevant source of information. In order to make decisions based on this, they need knowledge of the broader context of the situation. In hierarchical structures, this knowledge was possessed by senior level managers to whom subordinates conveyed the information obtained. The network structure strives to equip its employees with the knowledge they need to make their own decisions. It should be knowledge that goes far beyond professional specialization concerning conditions and strategic priorities of functioning of the organization, expressing itself in the knowledge of the various aspects of the problem that is the subject of the decision, providing the appropriate breadth of view and the ability to synthesize.

Decentralization of decision-making power, provided the superior has confidence in the subordinates, motivates the latter to achievement and professional development, enhances creativity and susceptibility to change, fosters learning

9 T. Peters, *Liberation Management*, Pan Book, London 1993, p. 466.

10 S. Kowalewski, *Teoria struktury administracji państwowej*, PWN, Warszawa 1973, pp. 52–53.

11 H.A. Simon, *Działanie administracji*, PWN, Warszawa 1976.

and responds appropriately to changes in the environment. All of these positive effects can be expected when the organization is large, has a complex profile and diverse areas of activity, operates in a complex and changing environment and – last but not least – employs qualified employees who are in need of professional development. Thanks to decentralization, the effect of combining large-scale operations with flexibility was once gained in divisional structures, which at first seemed impossible. A. Jay notes, however, that this way of thinking is not the discovery of the 1960s, but it appeared a long time ago, as evidenced by the organizational structure developed by St. Dominic when he founded the Dominican Order.[12] Furthermore, practical confirmation of the effectiveness of decentralization under pressure of the environment may be an example of Shell's unusual reaction to the oil crisis of the 1970s. It was then unquestionable that the conditions of the crisis required increasing the degree of centralization of decisions. Meanwhile, Shell went the other way: they increased the freedom of their local units to make decisions, thereby distancing their competitors.

The mode of operation based on the horizontal flow of information, on which resources are distributed and task forces are formed, leads to the phenomenon of heterarchy, or parallelism and variability of power centres. The manager of a given team may be subordinate to his or her employee, who directs at the same time another team in which the manager participates as a doer. Heterarchy deprives the hierarchy of the basic characteristic of stability and uniformity of the power system. The hierarchy is based on the binary relationships of dependence and transitivity of the chain of command, expressed in the concept of stacking of management: if A is in power over B, and B over C, then A has power over C. Heterarchy means that manager A can have power over B, and B over C, but also C can have power over A. In heterarchy, there is no dominating link. The mode of action is based on a horizontal flow of information; on this basis resources are distributed and task teams are deployed.[13]

The myth of informational restraint

Conventional wisdom includes the belief that the selection of information given to subordinates is a basis of the art of managing people. It is therefore assumed that the manager should not give everything he learns to his subordinates. This view is typically justified by two arguments. The first refers to the so-called

---

12 A. Jay, *Machiavelli i zarządzanie*, PWE, Warszawa 1996, p. 83.

13 G. Hedlund, *The Hypermodern MNC: A Heterarchy?*, Human Resources Management, No. 25, 1986.

phenomenon of information noise that arises as a result of excess of information. This excess makes it difficult for an employee to separate the information needed to complete a task from redundant information, as well as more important from less important. Therefore, the manager should inform the subordinate only about matters strictly related to the tasks he performs. Otherwise, when giving too much information to a subordinate, he may cause information noise, which makes it difficult to perform the task correctly.

While the above argument can be considered an attempt at a rational approach to the problem of communication between superiors and subordinates, the latter is a typical manifestation of paternalism. Selecting information before passing it on to subordinates is justified also by the fact that not all information is intended for people at lower levels of power. According to this view, a manager should not talk to subordinates about things which might cause them anxiety, emotional distress or a sense of danger. Any information about the anticipated troubles and difficulties facing the organization can demobilize and demoralize subordinates and make them think of issues they have no influence on, instead of focusing on their tasks. Unlike subordinates, the manager knows how to deal with this information because he is wiser and more mature. An obvious conclusion follows that subordinates should not be allowed this information, because as more foolish and immature they will not know what to do with it. This situation resembles the relationship between parents and their minor children.

In a decentralized organization, the manager must be primarily an informant to his subordinates who are often high-level specialists in a variety of fields. He cannot keep any information to himself because he is unable to assess which information and to what extent the employee will need to solve problems independently. The selection of information in this case does not belong to the manager, but to subordinates. It is they who, while representing various professional specialties, can only properly assess the suitability of the information in carrying out their assigned tasks. Decentralization of power involves intense communication and stimulating subordinates to learn and innovate. It was only in the old organizations that when executing simple, routine tasks the manager could know in advance what information each of his subordinates needed.

As for the second argument, the manager who is trying to protect the employees from disturbing information and claims at the same time that he supports partnership relations with subordinates is simply a hypocrite. Such a manager does it in order to save himself the trouble, and not to solve difficult problems together with his subordinates. It is impossible to manage people in this way in modern organizations. An outstanding manager, Lee Iacocca, treated communication in the organization as an ability to speak the truth. Departing from the truth or being silent about it is unacceptable in the relationship of the manager with subordinates. Truthfulness of the superior must go hand in hand with the ability to inspire subordinates, which is linked to trust.[14] The famous Churchill promise of "blood, sweat and tears" not only did not cause panic, but it was a powerful force mobilizing British society, because the prime minister enjoyed a great deal of social trust and, importantly, himself trusted the civic initiatives. Building a culture of "information sharing" is characteristic for organizations that recognize their employees as a key success factor. These organizations seek to create intellectual capital, where the communication system is crucial in addition to competence and, in particular, the forms of communication relevant to relationships between the superiors and the subordinates. This culture suppresses the distance of power, fosters a common vision of the functioning and development of the organization and ensures subordinates' involvement in solving management problems. Admittedly, for people with authoritarian personalities, this is not an encouraging vision.

3 The effects of the information revolution and globalization

The information revolution, launched in the last quarter of the twentieth century, with its ease of communication and the flexibility of manufacturing systems, has resulted in a significant acceleration of globalization. Globalization of markets leads, on one hand, to the large field of business activity and, on the other hand, to a denser concentration of this field, in which the influence, interests and forms of activity of the various organizations interpenetrate. As a result, the boundaries of the organizational systems are blurred and their forms are temporary. In place of uncertainty in management, thus far generated mainly by the internal work processes in the company, there is much greater uncertainty generated by customers, competitors and cooperants and the economic and sociocultural processes in world markets. This requires a change in the traditional paradigm of the organization and the application of new management approaches that, under the complex conditions of the socioeconomic environment and the complexity of the organization itself, cannot be based on mechanistic and deterministic assumptions. They must take utmost account of the discontinuity of socioeconomic processes and associated uncertainty. Globalization has resulted in the rapid saturation of markets and a significant increase in competition. The need to quickly adapt to the changing needs of customers and face competition

14 L. Iacocca (with C. Whitney), *Where Have All the Leaders Gone?*, Scribner, New York 2007, p. 8.

has fundamentally changed the strategy of many businesses. These strategies have clearly shifted the emphasis from quantitative to qualitative goals, from mass and big lot production to short run and piece production. More important than performance was the reaction time to market situations. Maximum flexibility, expressed in ease of making changes in the design and assortment of manufactured goods or services, and in the form and timing of their delivery to customers, is often a condition for survival. This involves not only adaptive changes, adjusting the company to the changing environment, but also changes in anticipating situations in the environment, creating a chance to gain an advantage over competitors. More than ever, the ability to innovate and the speed of adaptation to new conditions began to be counted on. In response to the dynamics of the environment and the speed of events, there is need for self-dynamics and the company's ability to evolve. Modern managers are therefore required to keep track of what is going on in the business environment.

A modern company, and even more the company of the future, appears as an organization constantly looking for its place in the market and development opportunities. Times of calm and rhythmic production for an increasing number of companies seem to belong to the past. A characteristic feature of the operating conditions of enterprises is, therefore, uncertainty, which is the biggest challenge for the whole management system. This is the uncertainty generated primarily by the environment rather than by the unpredictable behaviour of the members of the organization.

A form of response of enterprises to these determinants is to move from integration of the manufacturing process together with the support and service processes within a single company, to integration of these processes within the corporate network. The concept of the network is related both to the type of organizational structure of the company as well as to the way of management and the forms of business cooperation. This latter significance is fundamental as the business cooperation network decides on internal organizational solutions. Collaboration within the network allows for efficient operation in a climate of high complexity and uncertainty. However, this generally requires the use of similar solutions within the enterprise, consisting of dividing it into a large number of small and thus mobile and flexible organizational units, easily entering the network of diverse external relations.

Change is the main imperative in managing a modern enterprise. Improving performance by stabilizing operations, so characteristic of the peak of industrial civilization, has given way to the need to respond quickly to changes in the business environment. And in the global market, the pace of these changes is getting faster and faster. To take advantage of short-term opportunities and avoid constantly new threats, companies must constantly reshape their own relationships with the environment, their organizational structures and organizational procedures, and how they can perform management functions. The disintegration of large enterprises into small organizational units with great decision-making autonomy is considered in these conditions to be the only opportunity to face the growing wave of change. By justifying this point of view, the following benefits of small organizations are typically pointed to: faster response to customer needs through direct contact, higher product quality by focusing on a narrower profile, lower operating costs thanks to a simple and maximally slim line structure and better management thanks to intensive communication between all participants in the organizational system.[15]

T. Peters gives many examples of such disintegration of enterprises. For example, such a colossus of heavy industry as ABB was divided into 5000 profit centres, largely self-contained, each employing no more than several dozen people. Another example is the McKinsey consulting firm, which is a large but completely atomized organization, divided into hundreds of teams, of several or at most over a dozen of employees, of variable composition, working directly with clients. These design teams combine representatives from different professional backgrounds, and often representatives from different companies. The idea of the functioning of these teams is the continuous mobility of employees seeking the best possible job and new tasks.[16]

T. Peters draws attention to the apparent paradoxes of the functioning of the enterprise in network structures. On one hand, these companies become smaller, abandoning many tasks and subcontracting them and, on the other hand, becoming larger by participating in an extensive network of global cooperation. These companies are subject to internal disintegration, dividing into sets of small organizational units, conducting an independent activity in their environment, yet on the contrary – businesses are strongly integrated internally due to the need for the intensive exchange of resources and information between these entities.[17]

Contemporary leadership concepts boil down to the seemingly paradoxical statement that the leader giving up power to his subordinates actually increases his power. The greater the autonomy of workers, the greater the scope of social control, which is much more effective than managerial control. The greater the

---

15 P. McGovern, *The Network Corporation*, Chief Executive, April 1990.

16 T. Peters, *Liberation Management*, op. cit., pp. 132–136.

17 Ibidem, p. 473.

autonomy, the more employees feel the real impact on the functioning of the organization. This leads not only to greater motivation to work, but also makes them more susceptible to influence by colleagues and leaders. The best way to increase the impact on employees is to increase their independence.

Tomorrow's leader will have little in common with those who are still leading today. Some authors call him a leader who does not directly manage the actions of other people, but rather works with them to achieve common goals, who thinks with and not for people. Under the conditions of an information civilization, the leader in the organization should be primarily an agent of cultural change, which brings him closer to a teacher helping people to define goals and tasks, raising awareness of the effects of cultural change, contributing to the analysis and resolution of group and individual problems.[18] H.P. Sims and Ch.C. Manz go even further in their Self-Leadership concept. They call a super leader someone who gradually empowers his subordinates, providing them with first-class roles on the scene of the organization's operations while staying himself in the background.

The concept of self-leadership is at the opposite end of the classical spectrum. It is not so much about exerting influence on others as on oneself; it refers not to the relationship between leader and subordinates, but between equal leaders. H. P. Sims and Ch.C. Manz therefore do not share the fears of proponents of the organic concept of organizational paralysis in the absence of a clearly defined leader. Leaders are many – most employees are leaders. All of them with their knowledge, skills and ingenuity are the pillars of the organization and not just one leader. The effects of the information revolution have shaken belief in one-man leadership as a central organizational process. Many authors point to the need to look for other factors that better explain the nature of organizational events.[19]

The result of these tendencies was the emergence of a completely new type of organization, completely self-governing and without a hierarchy. In organizations whose strategy is to drift freely from one occasion to another, and the division of labour is fluid, the unique capabilities of employees are best utilized. The boss and strict formalization are replaced by the direct arrangements of co-operating people who have a sense of self-fulfilment. F. Laloux names such organizations "turquoise" and analyzes, among others, cases of companies from

18 R.F. Allen, J. Allen, Ch. Kraft, B. Certner, *The Organizational Unconscious*, "Human Resources Institute", Morristown 1987, pp. 86–90.

19 See, e.g.: J.R. Meindl, S.B. Ehrich, J.M. Dukerich, *The Romance of Leadership*, "Administrative Science Quarterly", 1985, No. 1.

different industries, such as the American energy company AES, the French FAVI foundry, the American Morning Star in the food industry and the Dutch company Buurtzorg, which employs environmental nurses.[20]

4 Ethical, rational and diffused leadership

In the age of information civilization, a radical departure from authoritarian leadership is necessary. This is determined by the effects of the technical revolution and the accompanying educational revolution. In order to appropriately utilize new technical possibilities and new intellectual capital in modern organizations, ethical, rational and diffused leadership should be sought.

4.1 Ethical leadership

Ethical leadership requires a fundamental change in the relationship between the manager and the subordinates. Instead of an instrumental relation to subordinates, justifying the use of dictation and manipulation, it is necessary to have a subjective relation where the manager shortens the distance of power and treats his subordinates as equal partners. The subjective relation is based on the belief that subordinates have some potential that could be used for the needs of the organization and – which is especially important – that should be developed. Peter Drucker is credited with claiming that a good manager is known not for being a better expert than his subordinates, but for being able to use their potential. The subjective relation began to spread with the development of participatory management methods. It has been pointed out that the involvement of subordinates in solving problems, hitherto reserved for managers, significantly increases their motivation and results in improved organizational effectiveness. The decisive factor for the process of moving away from the traditional way of understanding power is the influence of an ever-changing and unpredictable environment of an organization that changes established relationships of power, imposing on all employees an obligation to deal with the uncertainty generated by this environment. This leads to temporary and interchangeable organizational roles and situational management, where the division into managers and subordinates is often obliterated.

Subjective relation to subordinates also requires respecting their cultural habits and values that appear to be unfavourable from the point of view of

20 F. Laloux, *Pracować inaczej. Nowatorski model organizacji inspirowany kolejnym etapem rozwoju ludzkiej świadomości*, Studio EMKA, Warszawa 2015.

organizational goals. Respect, as T. Reilly observes, strengthens trust because it is based on the belief that others may also be right. Expressing respect encourages those to whom it is addressed to maintain contacts and openness to arguments.[21] Managers who respect their subordinates allow them to be themselves, to create their own needs and beliefs. They follow the basic moral principle of Immanuel Kant, according to which people should be treated as a goal, never as a means to an end. Peter Senge quotes Max de Pree, the retired president of a large company, who speaks of the need for a special pact between the individual and the manager representing the organization. This pact should consist of a shared commitment to ideas, problems, values, goals and management processes. Relations between people in the organization, based on mutual respect and respect for dignity have, according to him, a sacred character.[22]

The expression of this point of view was Robert Greenleaf's concept, presented in the 1970s, and somewhat provocatively called Service Leadership. This kind of leadership reverses traditional relations: it is not that the subordinates are for the manager, but the manager is for the subordinates. Therefore, he should focus on their needs and help them develop their potential so that they gain not only more knowledge and skills, but become more independent. The servant leader is trying to minimize the instruments of formal authority, replacing them with the ability to listen, empathize and unconditionally accept people who have different views than his own.[23] Of course, "servility" has a rather peculiar meaning in this case; it is not about subordinating the manager to his subordinates, but only to their development needs. It is in accordance with the well-known view of Peter Drucker that the better a manager is, the more he can develop and exploit the potential of his subordinates.

4.2 Rational leadership

In the 1980s, the concept of transformational leadership emerged. It was an attempt to respond to the increasing frequency of changes in contemporary organizations caused by increasingly complex and changing environmental conditions. Transformational leadership makes change management the central axis of management. It is rightly assumed that, in order to quickly and effectively change

21 T. Reilly, *Respect Builds Trust*, Industrial Distribution, No. 8, 2002

22 P.E. Senge, *Piąta dyscyplina. Teoria i praktyka organizacji uczących się*, Dom Wydawniczy ABC, Warszawa 1998, p 150.

23 R.K. Greenleaf, *Servant Leadership: A Journey into the Nature of Legitimate Power and Greatness*, Paulist, New York 1977.

an organization – specifically the organizational culture – the people should be changed in the first place. Otherwise resistance to change, resulting from attachment to cultural stereotypes, can effectively thwart reformers' plans. What kind of manager does not have a problem with changing the culture of subordinates and never gets resistance from them? The answer is obvious: a charismatic leader. In this way, a correct assumption led to a completely incorrect conclusion about the need to return to the concept of a charismatic leader in the context of globalization and the information revolution, where this concept particularly strikes one as anachronistic.

It was easier said than done, because charismatic leaders are few and far between. Proponents of the concept, however, decided that it was enough for the managers to try to assimilate at least some of the characteristics of charismatic leaders and to take care of their authority. Helpful, among others, were the examples of the behaviour of outstanding managers, whose biographies, achievements and memories began to be intensively published at that time. The effect, probably not intended, was the idealization of managers, who, among other things, found expression in exaggerated emphasis on their role in modern society and thus justified their gigantic and fast-growing earnings. A.K. Koźmiński writes about this, drawing attention to the ease with which a belief in one's own capabilities and the infallibility of decisions is gaining popularity in the managerial environment. Managers' megalomania and their nonchalant attitude towards clients are becoming the most serious threats to the organization.[24]

Transformational management should therefore be considered a step backwards from the earlier concept of participatory management. Again, we are dealing with an increase in the distance of power and the transformation of subordinates into obedient performers of the orders of brilliant superiors. As before, the basis of the leader's authority becomes admiration for the brilliant accomplishments of the boss, not inspiration of the subordinates for independence and development. Probably many practitioners and theorists of management would agree with A. Stachowicz-Stanusch's view that the duty of a leader is to act brightly in order to transform a group of individuals into an engaged community.[25] From the point of view of the principles of liberal democracy, and transferred to the management of organizations, you can only agree with

---

24 A.K. Koźmiński, *Koniec świata menedżerów*, Wydawnictwa Menedżerskie i Profesjonalne, Warszawa 2008, pp 107–109.

25 A. Stachowicz-Stanusch, *Zarządzanie poprzez wartości. Perspektywa rozwoju współczesnego przedsiębiorstwa*, Wydawnictwo Politechniki Śląskiej, Gliwice 2004, p. 25.

this, when the brilliant leader makes his subordinates equally brilliant, not just devoted to him. This is only possible with a rational leader who uses education, never with an emotional one who uses indoctrination.

The leader may try to perpetuate his superior position and the influence on the behaviour of subordinates, using their needs for security and certainty, his own personality traits and the fascination they generate in the people who are willing to subjugate to him. However, the goal of the leader can be quite different. Utilizing his authority, he can influence subordinates to become more and more self-reliant in their behaviour and independent of him in satisfying their need for security and certainty. By acting in this way, the leader consciously restricts his own leadership, which after some time only boils down to coordinating the work of independent and creative performers. So, based on this, we can distinguish emotional leadership, preserving the relationships of superiority and subordination, in which the leader satisfies the basic subsistence needs of subordinates that include the sense of certainty and security; and the rational leadership that teaches subordinates to meet their needs and transform their leadership relationships into coordination relations. The lack of recognition of these two forms of governance is probably a source of many misunderstandings about leadership. Something others have in mind are those who see leadership as the path to subordinates' autonomy, and the relationship of superiority and subordination as temporary in nature, and something else – those who see the essence of leadership in the permanence of a big social distance between the leader and the subordinate that results from the difference in "human format."

Employee development can be ensured only by a reasonable leader, never by an emotional one. It is not possible for a charismatic leader who flourishes above the others to be accompanied by the blossoming of the potential of his subordinates. And it is not because the self-cantered leader will consciously or unconsciously dampen the development of others to prevent them from threatening his position, but because the subordinates, who admire their leader, do not want that development themselves. For subordinates to thrive, the leader must step down from the pedestal, and he must also lose the monopoly on formulating captivating visions and raising brilliant ideas. It is not only about decentralization of decisions; it is about decentralization of wisdom, prestige and the need for self-realization.

A rational leader commands moderate respect. None of his subordinates question the leader's knowledge and skills, or consider him infallible. This type of leader is often annoying because he stubbornly makes demands and forces his subordinates to think. Such a leader does not raise strong emotions. The subordinates neither fear him nor adore him; he has no qualities of a folk hero.

After years, his subordinates have a little awareness of how large this leader's influence was on their further professional achievements. This influence did not result from the fact that the leader had revealed professional secrets before them, but because he had forced them to discover them independently. It was understood long ago by the wise Chinese Lao-tse when he wrote: "The best leaders are those whose existence people do not notice (...) When the best leader finishes his job, people say –"We did it ourselves."[26]

4.3 Diffused leadership

Taking into account modern civilization concepts, the future of organizational power is best expressed by the definition of Andrzej Koźmiński, in which leadership is understood as organizational, not personal potential. This author writes: "Speaking of leadership, we will therefore have in mind an important resource of the organization, an element of its social potential: the sum of the capacity, skills and talents to influence members of the organization by the other members of this organization to achieve the goals of the organization."[27]

With this understanding, the leader disappears as a specific person endowed with special characteristics that allow him to significantly influence the behaviour of other people. Leadership skills can be diffused and time-sensitive. In different situations and circumstances, members of the organization mutually interact with each other in the process of achieving organizational goals. The direction of these interactions does not need to be in line with the formal relations of superiority and subordination. For example, one of the members of the team comes up with the idea of solving a problem that has appeared in their work. The idea is gaining widespread approval, and members of the team are beginning to realize it. At other times, someone else in this team will come up with a solution that will be considered helpful in achieving success. Team members will remain under his influence to such an extent and as long as it is needed to gain the expected benefits.

The dispersion of knowledge in the organizational system causes that the superiors are no longer able, as they once were, to know the details of the work of their subordinates. What is more, they will not be able to decide about this job. But as this work becomes more and more complex, the workers must cooperate

26 Quot. after: M. Krokowski, P. Rydzewski, *Zarządzanie emocjami*, Imperia, Łódź 2002, p. 96.

27 A.K. Koźmiński, *Zarządzanie w warunkach niepewności*, Wydawnictwo Naukowe PWN, Warszawa 2004, p. 151.

closely and take responsibility for the entire organization, not just for their section. In this way, P.F. Drucker imagines the functioning of a knowledge-based organization, where "there are no 'subordinates', and there are only collaborating individuals."[28]

It can be assumed that under these circumstances, the management processes in organizational systems will be characterized by:

- Resignation from the principle of hierarchy,
- Transiency and volatility of managerial functions,
- Democratization of the process of formulating the vision of the organization and decision-making.

The principle of hierarchy could be sufficient in a relatively stable and less complex environment of the organization. Everything, however, indicates that the environment will be getting increasingly changeable and varied. Instead of the hierarchy, different forms of horizontal coordination of activities will be needed to ensure the required level of integration, by increasing the flexibility and adaptability of the organizational system. Horizontal coordination serves to multiply the ways of cooperation between workers, which on one hand increases the adaptability of the system, but on the other hand becomes a source of uncertainty due to the emergence of difficulties in defining one's own place and role in the organization. The value of cooperation increases as the organization's democratization progresses. As a result of the dispersal of decision-making powers, all members can, at least theoretically, participate, though obviously unequally, in the exercise of power. Under these conditions, the role of horizontal ties grows, and the need for control, so characteristic of hierarchical systems, is replaced by trust. The primary task of the manager is to facilitate effective collaboration between people and to clear up information channels. Leadership based on trust leads to increased employee motivation, creativity and openness to innovation.

Transience and volatility of management functions prejudge the rational foundations of the manager's authority. A temporary manager is a person who has the knowledge and skills appropriate to the nature of the task and the conditions of its implementation, as well as the experience and personality traits that may prove particularly useful in carrying out a specific task here and now. It also means that the management will be shared by almost all employees, whose unique characteristics and skills can be used at different times in the process. In

28 P.F. Drucker, *Społeczeństwo pokapitalistyczne*, Wydawnictwo Naukowe PWN, Warszawa 1999, p. 91.

the future, employees will not occupy the manager's position permanently, as in most contemporary organizations, but they will be managers from time to time. Therefore, it will not be possible to maintain a cultural pattern which leads to treating the situation of losing a managerial position in terms of personal failure. Such an approach is anachronistic in the conditions of functioning of task teams in network structures. Team managers change as needed in task implementation. Permanent attachment to a managerial position is therefore not possible, and its acquisition or loss cannot be assessed in terms of success or failure. It is worth noting, however, that thanks to the autonomy granted, every employee of this type of organization becomes, in a sense, a manager of implementation of his or her own tasks. The term coined by American authors H. Simms and Ch. Manz – "self-leadership" – is by all means justified here.

Democratization of the organization's vision and decision-making essentially limits the scope of managerial power and shortens the social distance between him and his subordinates. These are the processes in which all team members will participate as high-quality professionals. Every decision requires a rational justification, which the manager owes to his co-workers.

All indications are that in the organizations of the future the power structure will be poorly developed, and at the same time the following traits will be dominant: impulsiveness, improvisation and risk-taking tendencies in pursuing the needs of customers. There is no doubt that these organizations will thrive and gain advantage over their competitors not through ingenious leaders, but by exploiting their entire intellectual capital. They will depend on their talented and knowledgeable employees whose aspirations will have to be recognized, which should be reflected in the creation of new career models.

The activity of the future, although in some organizations already existing, managers is so far away from the managerial tasks we are accustomed to, that perhaps it is worth replacing the term "manager," not to mention "leader," with a more modest one but better reflecting the character of this activity. This term can be "coordinator," whose operation mainly consists of receiving information from the environment, handing it over to employees, facilitating group and individual communication, sending messages and integrating incoming responses. It is therefore primarily a social communication activity aimed at the continuous learning process of the organization.

The future form of the organizational power relation seems to be, therefore, democratic coordination, conditioned by the autonomy and entrepreneurship of employees. Employees have a wide range of decision-making powers and the ensuing responsibility. The coordinator decides about the way to use the results of work of individual performers rather than about how they work. The coordinator does not interfere with the matters of task performers in which they are professionals, although he may present his remarks and ideas to them. Also, task performers may submit their own points of view in matters reserved to the coordinator's decision.

Democratic coordination becomes the primary form of governance in virtual organizations that develop network structures. In the global market, previously unknown forms of organization, such as company, are increasingly appearing, which employs only one person – the president, acting as the coordinator, organizing a dynamic network of cooperation with representatives of other companies. The added value of this company is determined by the creativity of its president – the coordinator and his ability to use the creativity of other network participants.

How it will be in the future is, of course, unknown. The presented model of organizational power should, however, be regarded as reassuring, as it unveils the blessed twilight of emotional leadership, the leadership that enslaves subordinates, often unfortunately with their full approval.

References

Allen R.F., Allen J., Kraft Ch., Certner B., *The Organizational Unconscious*, Human Resources Institute, Morinstown 1987.

Drucker P.F., *Społeczeństwo pokapitalistyczne*, Wydawnictwo Naukowe PWN, Warszawa 1999.

Fromm E., *Anatomia ludzkiej destrukcyjności*, Dom Wydawniczy Rebis, Poznań 2002.

Greenleaf R.K., *Servant Leadership: A Journey into the Nature of Legitimate Power and Greatness*, Paulist, New York 1977.

Harmon F.G., Jacobs G., *The Vital Difference. Unleashing the Powers of Sustained Corporate Success*, New York, 1985, http://mirainterational.com/books/difference/CHAPO 1.htm.

Hedlund G., *The Hypermodern MNC: A Heterarchy?*, Human Resources Management, No. 25, 1986, 9–35.

Iaccoca L. (with C. Whitney), *Where Have All the Leaders Gone?*, Scribner, New York 2007.

Jay A., *Machiavelli i zarządzanie*, PWE, Warszawa 1996.

Krokowski M., Rydzewski P., *Zarządzanie emocjami*, Imperia, Łódź 2002.

Kowalewski S., *Teoria struktury administracji państwowej*, PWN, Warszawa 1973.

Koźmiński A.K., *Zarządzanie w warunkach niepewności*, Wydawnictwo Naukowe PWN, Warszawa 2004.

Koźmiński A.K., *Koniec świata menedżerów*, Wydawnictwa Menedżerskie i Profesjonalne, Warszawa 2008.

Laloux F., *Pracować inaczej. Nowatorski model organizacji inspirowany kolejnym etapem rozwoju ludzkiej świadomości*, Studio EMKA, Warszawa 2015.

Manent P., *Intelektualna historia liberalizmu*, Arcana, Kraków 1994.

McClelland D., *The Two Faces of Power*, Journal of International Affairs, No. 24(1)., 1970, 29–47.

McGovern P., *The Network Corporation*, Chief Executive, April 1990, 67–80.

Meindl J.R., Ehrich S.B., Dukerich J.M., *The Romance of Leadership*, Administrative Science Quarterly, Vol. 30, No. 1, 1985. 78–102.

Montesquie, *O duchu praw*, chapter XI, Książka i Wiedza, Warszawa 1957.

Peters T., *Liberation Management*, Pan Book, London 1993.

Reilly T., *Respect Builds Trust*, Industrial Distribution, No. 91 (8), 2002, 132–141

Senge P.E., *Piąta dyscyplina. Teoria i praktyka organizacji uczącej się*, Dom Wydawniczy ABC, Warszawa 1998.

Simon H.A., *Działanie administracji*, PWN, Warszawa 1976.

Stachowicz-Stanusch A., *Zarządzanie poprzez wartości. Perspektywa rozwoju współczesnego przedsiębiorstwa*, Wydawnictwo Politechniki Śląskiej, Gliwice 2004.

Ury N.I., Brett J.M., Goldberg S.B., *Getting Disputes Resolved*, Jossey-Bass, San Francisco 1988.

Wang K.Y., Clegg S., *Trust and Decision Making: Are Managers Different in the People's Republic of China and in Australia?*, Cross Cultural Management. An International Journal 9(1): 30–45, 2002.

Werner Auer-Rizzi, Gerhard Reber, Jerzy Mączyński, Łukasz Prysiński, and Dariusz Wyspiański

Social Partnership: Comparisons between Managers in Four Countries Based on the Vroom/Yetton Model

Abstract: The authors analyse the Vroom/Yetton leadership model and present its application in four countries: Austria, the Czech Republic, Germany, and Poland. The cross-cultural research has been done to present social partnership in the countries mentioned. It proves the Vroom/Yetton model could help to support effective leadership in social sciences.

Keywords: leadership, intercultural differences, Vroom/Yetton model, cross-cultural research, social partnership

I Attempts to differentiate intercultural differences in leadership behavior

Twenty years after the first edition of his book *Culture's Consequences* in 1980, Geert Hofstede looked back and mentioned that "after a slow start the book has become a classic and one of the most cited sources in the entire Social Science Citation Index" (Hofstede, 2001, XVII). Although Hofstede refers to all social sciences, the collection of his data was concentrated on the management of one multinational computer company (IBM). For the first edition, he collected from 1967 to 1973 answers from almost 117,000 employees in 66 countries (Hofstede, 1980, 54) with a questionnaire containing four measures (power distance, uncertainty avoidance, individualism, masculinity). In the second edition (Hofstede, 2001), he expanded the questionnaire – in cooperation with Bond (Bond, 1992) – with the dimension "long- versus short-term orientation," and added 23 countries including Poland (Hofstede, 2001, 356 ff).

It is no wonder that this study found the mentioned worldwide attraction and stimulated the attention for similar studies in the area of management. Among them, Robert House started a comparable giant study, the so-called GLOBE-Project, which was based on Hofstede's pattern. The project started in 1992 with the GLOBE coordinating team consisting of five members (House, 2004, XXXIII). Overall, 170 investigators from 62 cultures worked in the project, and questionnaires from 17,300 managers in 951 organizations in three industries (financial services, food processing, telecommunications) were collected. In total, the study used nine dimensions (performance orientation, future orientation, gender egalitarianism, assertiveness, individualism and collectivism, power distance, humane orientation, uncertainty avoidance) and the results were published in two books with 1880 pages (House et al., 2004; Javidan et al., 2007).

Despite the closeness of both concepts, the authors ran into a grim fight about their application of quantitative measurements (Javidan et al., 2006; Hofstede, 2006). This clash of "two elephants" (Smith, 2006) did not find recognition in the literature, because the real problems of both studies are their dependence on self-report questionnaires (Taras et al., 2009; 2010).

Reber and Szabo were invited to represent Austria in the GLOBE study (Reber & Szabo, 2007). Szabo (2007) started, before the battle between House and Hofstede was published, a different evaluation of the model. She was stimulated by Michael Agar (1996), who, in the beginning of the GLOBE project, was a member of the coordinating team responsible for qualitative research methods. But as these methods were not used in the final design, Agar left the project. Szabo (2007) started a qualitative study in five countries (Czech Republic, Finland, Poland, Sweden, and Austria) based on quantitative investigations including the event management model of Smith and Peterson (1988; Smith et al., 1994) and the Vroom and Yetton (1973) model. She came to the conclusion that the "… country indices originating from the Vroom/Yetton study … are in large part in line with the qualitative findings" (Szabo, 2007, 289). This result lead us back to continue our interest in the application of the Vroom/Yetton model for cross-cultural research, which was started as a cooperative endeavor of Jago, Reber, and Böhnisch (1986).

II The Vroom/Yetton leadership model

The Vroom/Yetton leadership model comprises four elements, which are interconnected: (1) leadership strategies, (2) diagnostic questions, (3) decision rules, and (4) case sets for data collection.

1 Leadership strategies

The basic idea was the assumption that the participation of workers increased the quality of decision-making processes (Coch and French, 1948; Katz, Maccoby, & Morse, 1950). Doubts arose in experiments in a Norwegian factory, in which no significant differences were found between the performance in a situation with participation and without (French et al., 1960; Vroom, 1960; Miller and Monge, 1986). It became obvious that the "... effect of participation on decision quality depends on certain observable features of the decision-making situations. It depends on where the relevant knowledge or experience resides, that is, in the leader, the group, or both. It depends on the goals of the potential participants, particularly on the extent to which group or team members support the organizational objectives embedded in the problem. Finally, the amount of synergy exhibited in the team-based process depends on the skills and abilities of team members in working together effectively in solving problems" (Vroom, 2000, 85).

Also time constraints limit the extent of participative processes. Based on the ideas of Maier (1963), Vroom and Yetton (1973) summarize participativeness in the formula:

Leadership Effectiveness (LE) is a function of Quality (Q) multiplied by Acceptance (A).

The literature of participation discussed the different intensities of participation. For example, Tannenbaum and Schmidt (1995) distinguished seven grades, varying in the influence by the leader and the intensity of the influence of subordinates. Vroom and Yetton (1973) reduced this differentiation. According to them, a leader can choose from five levels of participation with the terms AI, AII, CI, CII, and GII – A stands for autocratic decisions, C for consultation, and G for group decision. The assignment of different participation scores for the strategies between the extremes of the scale (AI = 0; GII = 10) is based on empirical studies in which managers rated the distances on a 1 to 10 scale.

2 Leadership situation – diagnostic questions

Each leadership situation is characterized by a combination of seven attributes. Each one of these attributes is represented by a diagnostic question, which can be answered with yes or no. Three of the attributes refer to the quality dimensions of the decision to be made, and four of them to the acceptance/commitment dimension. (A) Does the problem possess a quality requirement? (B) Does the leader have sufficient information to make a high-quality decision? (C) Is the problem structured? (D) Is acceptance of decision by subordinates important for effective implementation? (E) Will an autocratic decision made by the leader be accepted by subordinates? (F) Do subordinates share the organizational goals to be attained in solving this problem? (G) Is conflict among subordinates over preferred solutions likely?

3 Decision rules

The decision rules exclude certain strategies in certain leadership situations (characterized above). The model provides seven rules (Leader Information Rule, Goal Congruence Rule, Unstructured Problem Rule, Acceptance Rule, Conflict Rule, Fairness Rule, Acceptance Priority Rule), the first three protecting the quality dimension, and the latter four the acceptance/commitment dimension of effective decisions. Each rule *excludes* certain decision strategies in specific situations. The Leader Information Rule, for example, eliminates strategy AI (autocratic decision making) from being feasible in a situation, where the quality of the decision is important (diagnostic question A = "yes") and the leader does not have enough information or expertise to solve the problem alone (diagnostic question B = "no").

The result of applying all seven rules to a decision situation is called a "feasible set" for that situation. In other words, the set shows which strategies are still feasible in this particular situation after applying all the relevant rules. When the feasible set contains more than one strategy, there are additional criteria to focus on just one strategy – one for time saving ("Model A") and one for subordinate education ("Model B"). The latter selects the most participative feasible strategy which provides great involvement of subordinates in decision-making and more opportunities to enhance their managerial, technical, and team skills.

Simon (1990) and Kahneman (2002) remind scientists and practitioners of a "bounded rationality." As part of this concept, the whole model concentrates its "building blocks" to the limits on the capacity of information processing, the "magical number seven", plus or minus two (Miller, 1956; 1994). The combination of the dimension strategies, diagnostic questions, and decision rules are presented in a decision tree, which can be found in all textbooks in the area of organizational behavior. Such a "summary" demonstrated the reduction of complexity of leadership decision-making and increased its "relevance" for researchers and practitioners. The model does not pretend to have the only solution/recommendation for all leadership problems. Vroom and Jago (1978), Magerison and Glube (1979), and Field (1982) validated the Vroom/Yetton Model and Böhnisch et al. (1987) demonstrated its intercultural validity.

4 Case sets for data collection and its application

Instead of questionnaires the data are collected by administering a problem set of 30 one-page cases. The individual cases for the problem set were "… selected and rewritten from actual descriptions of real decisions provided to the author from hundreds of managers" (Vroom and Yetton, 1973, 98). The problem sets were validated in the USA by Vroom/Yetton (1973), and in Germany/Austria by Böhnisch (1991) in a multifactorial experimental design, which demonstrated its relevance for typical problems and decisions by managers.

This form of data collection follows a "close-to-action" approach, in contrast to a "far-from-action" approach, which does not "... stress general subconscious needs, motives, and values" (Locke and Latham, 1990, 6). This approach is targeted at the complex experiences about the learning of leadership, which was collected from childhood on and is stored in the area of "tacit knowledge" (Wagner and Sternberg, 1985).

III The application of the Vroom/Yetton model in Austria, Czech Republic, Germany, and Poland

Since 1985 the data collection with the Vroom/Yetton model was done in 13 countries, and included the four countries which are the focus of this chapter. The problem set was administered to managers, who, at the time of data collection, were unfamiliar with the Vroom/Yetton model. In addition to the cases, they only received the definition of the five strategies and were asked to select one for each of the 30 cases. As this was the usual procedure for all studies of the program, the data for Austrian, German, and Czech managers were collected prior to leadership training programs. In this situation, the respondents were not providing a "favor" to the researchers since their main concern was the improvement of their leadership skills in a training program. We expect that with this procedure the "Hawthorne Effect" could be minimized. In this program the participants got an explanation of the Vroom/Yetton model and feedback about their individual behavior and a summary of their groups. We applied this procedure to the Austrian, Czech, and (West-)German managers, and the Polish data with the Vroom/Yetton model were collected by Maczynski in 1994 and 1996 before the GLOBE project was published (Maczynski et al., 1994; Jago et al., 1996).

The collected data between 1985 and 2015 are summarized in a longitudinal study in Tab. 1. For the analysis of differences between the time periods we ran Oneway ANOVA with the time periods as independent variables, which represent the columns in Tab. 1. The dependent variables, which are represented in the different rows in Tab. 1, were the mean level of participation, the rate of agreement with the feasible set, violation rate of quality rules, and the violation rate of acceptance rules.

The results in Tab. 1 show that the mean level of participation in Austria and Germany reached a relatively high level until the year 2000, which, from 2001

Tab. 1: Longitudinal analysis of leadership behavior in Austria, Germany, Czech Republic, and Poland.

Period	85-90	91-95	96-00	01-05	06-10	11-15	ANOVA F-Value
Austrian Manager[1] n=	1016	927	1168	935	480	310	
Mean Level of Participation (MLP)	5,39^{c}	5,29^{c}	5,28^{c}	5,04^{b}	4,80^{a}	4,73^{a}	30,59***
% Agreement with Feasible Set	71,76^{cd}	71,66^{cd}	72,53^{d}	71,06^{bc}	70,22^{b}	68,96^{a}	12,05***
% Violations Quality Rules (R1-3)	16,09	15,85	15,47	16,05	16,11	16,84	n.s.
% Violations Acceptance Rules (R4-7)	31,37^{a}	31,85^{a}	30,56^{a}	33,95^{b}	35,19^{b}	38,60^{c}	19,44***
German Manager[1] n=		361	328	397	423	241	
Mean Level of Participation (MLP)		5,42 c	5,28 c	5,07 b	4,83 a	4,80 a	19,94***
% Agreement with Feasible Set		73,20 d	72,02 c	70,70 b	69,93 ab	69,35 a	13,47***
% Violations Quality Rules (R1-3)		14,92	14,74	14,79	15,45	15,42	n.s.
% Violations Acceptance Rules (R4-7)		29,53 a	32,38 b	35,29 c	36,80 c	37,13 c	17,17***
Czech Manager[2] n=		370	188	328	259	54	
Mean Level of Participation (MLP)		4,25 b	4,39 b	4,30 b	4,22 b	3,97 a	n.s.
% Agreement with Feasible Set		67,00 b	65,69 b	65,92 b	65,92 b	63,02 a	3,48**
% Violations Quality Rules (R1-3)		18,15 b	18,24 b	17,23 b	18,16 b	20,25 a	n.s.
% Violations Acceptance Rules (R4-7)		44,40 c	45,67 bc	47,23 abc	48,59 ab	50,62 a	4,52**
Polish Manager[3] n=	146	253			23	32	
Mean Level of Participation (MLP)	4,39	4,51			4,29	4,27	n.s.
% Agreement with Feasible Set	63,56	64,03			64,35	61,98	n.s.
% Violations Quality Rules (R1-3)	22,29	21,34			19,86	22,40	n.s.
% Violations Acceptance Rules (R4-7)	48,30	48,37			51,76	53,57	n.s.

* p < 0,05 ** = p < 0,01 *** p < 0,001

A significant F-value means that atleast one period is significantly different from the others. In addition, we ran the Duncan-Test to compare all periods against each other. The results of this test are shown with the superscripts after each mean value of the dependent variables. The periods for each dependent variable, which share the same superscript, do not significantly differ from each other.

Source: [1]data recalculated from 1985-2015 based on Auer-Rizzi and Reber (2007) - new data from 2006-2015 not yet published
[2]data recalculated from 1990-2013 based on Auer-Rizzi and Reber (2013) - new data from 2012-2013 not yet published
[3]data recalculated from 1990-2015 based on Jagoetal. (1996) - new data from 2008-2015 not yet published

on, constantly changed to lower degrees. Regarding Maier's (1963) formula of "leadership effectiveness," a most striking factor is that the emphasis on quality dimensions of decisions, given through a relative low number of violations of the quality rules, stays constant over the whole time span from 1985 to 2015. In contrast, the violation rate of acceptance rules stays constant in Austria until 2000 before it significantly increases, whereas in Germany this tendency starts one period earlier. The Czech and Polish managers started with low levels of participation and higher violation rates of acceptance rules in comparison to Germany and Austria, but with stable results over time. In general, we see a tendency of a decrease of partnership in all four countries.

The Vroom/Yetton model does not include hints about the driving forces of change or stability of behavioral patterns. We will interpret the development of leadership behavior using the framework of Douglas North, which gives us the opportunity to differentiate different levels of forces in the development of changes in societies and their economic performance. According to North (1990), change and adaption to situational demands can happen on the institutional, the organizational, and the individual level, which also influence each other.

> "Institutions are the rules of the game in a society or, more formally, are the humanly devised constraints that shape human interaction. In consequence they structure incentives in human exchange, whether political, social, or economic. Institutional change shapes the way societies evolve through time and hence is the key to understanding historic change" (North, 1990: 3).

North defines "formal" and "informal" elements as institutions: formal ones are constitutions, laws, and contracts; informal ones are social norms and beliefs, conventions and codes of conduct.

> "Organizations include political bodies (political parties, the Senate, a city council, a regulatory agency), economic bodies (firms, trade unions, family farms, cooperatives), social bodies (churches, clubs, athletic associations) and educational bodies (schools, universities, vocational training centers). They are groups of individuals bound by some common purpose to achieve objectives. Modeling organizations is analyzing governance structures, skills, and how learning by doing will determine the organization's success over time. Both which organizations come into existence and how they evolve are fundamentally influenced by the institutional framework. In turn they influence how the institutional framework evolves" (North, 1990: 5).

According to North (1996: 3), individual "[l]earning [...] is a cumulative process of cultural conditioning in which the experiences of each generation are filtered through the existing belief system and result in its incremental modification." The definitions demonstrate an existence of inertia within the different cultures. Furthermore, North differentiates the stability between the elements of his framework:

> "[T]he fundamental source of change is learning by entrepreneurs of organizations. [...] Change is typically incremental, reflecting ongoing ubiquitous evolving perceptions of the entrepreneurs of organizations in the context of an institutional matrix that is characterized by network externalities, complementarities and economies of scope among the existing organizations. Moreover, since the organizations owe their existence to the institutional matrix, they will be an ongoing interest group to assure the perpetuation of that institutional structure-- thus assuring path dependence. Revolutions do occur, however, when organizations with different interests emerge (typically as a result of dissatisfaction with the performance of existing organizations), and the fundamental conflict between organizations over institutional change cannot be mediated within the

> existing institutional framework. Path dependence means that history matters; that the choices we make today and tomorrow are constrained by the past evolution of the belief systems and institutions of the society" (North, 1996: 10 f).

Our presentation of social partnership in the four countries cannot give a complete history of the social partnerships, only relevant examples can be emphasized.

1 Austria

The first idea to stabilize Austria after the end of the Second World War was a wage-price agreement which was installed by the new federal government. But in 1950 this approach could not be sustained, once the workers started some riots because of price increases and wages lagging behind. This rebellion was enough to bring the memories back to the consequences of the civil war, and the first steps for a solid social partnership were started (Preinfalk, 2010, 8), which included the workers, farmers, and entrepreneurs. These groups became compulsory members of chambers of labor, agriculture, and commerce. (The bigger industrial companies are organized as members in the chamber of commerce and continued an older tradition to work together in the Foundation of Austrian Industry.) The chamber of labor supported the unions and also provided help for consumers. The health care system was led by the chamber of labor and the chamber of commerce. All organizations were connected to the party system, which represented their interests in the federal and provincial parliaments. Within the companies a hierarchy of works councils, differentiated for white and blue color employees, was installed. All these members of the system worked together in the so-called parity commission (Novotny, 1991).

In reference to North, the development in Austria did not include international forces and international relations. Both dimensions played a role five years later, when the allied forces left the country in a "peaceful revolution." The latter occurred when an Austrian government delegation visited Moscow. This trip culminated in the signing of the Moscow Memorandum on April 15, 1955, which expressly stated the readiness of the Soviet government to remove their troops if Austria would commit itself to permanent neutrality, to become a "… free and independent democratic state and to guarantee its independence in particular from any attempts to unite with Germany … [as well as] the limitation of Austria's military sovereignty in both of personnel and equipment …" (Austrian Parliament, 1989, 23–24). Even before April 1955, the Western powers had informed the Austrian government of their wish to follow the Soviet Union as soon as possible. The Moscow Memorandum was adopted by the Austrian

Nationalrat as part of the Austrian constitution on October 26, 1955, and this date was adopted as Austria's national holiday.

The social partnership and national sovereignty stabilized Austria and its economic and social development tremendously. Nevertheless, the system encountered different disparities in the quality of leadership, especially regarding the base concept of Maier's formula of the multiplication of quality and acceptance.

(1) In the period between 2000 and 2004 the liberal party replaced the social democrats in the federal government coalition. The liberals usurped a bank in an Austrian province, which collapsed relatively rapidly, and the federal government was responsible for the debts.
(2) Meanwhile the same happened with the fourth largest bank owned by the union, which "… got involved in financial speculations that ended in the disposal of the bank to foreign financial investors … to cover the losses" (Preinfalk, 2010, 13).
(3) It was possibly a rumor that a US officer reported in Washington that Austria, after the Second World War, would be the poorest country in Europe. This situation may explain why Austria got from the Marshall Plan (established by the USA 1947 with 14 billion US dollars) the highest share per capita after Norway. During the war, from 1938 on, the German government built a steel company in Linz, Austria. Its construction could not be finished before the end of the war. After the war 32 % of the Marshall Plan money was invested by the state of Austria into the completion of this project (Rathkolb, 2010, 900). The final construction and operation of the steel plant provided jobs. "In 1951 the company employed 9,316 blue collar workers, 1,874 white collar workers and 399 apprentices with a turnover of 1,660 million Schilling (550 million for the export). Already in 1952, the total export brought 944.2 million Schillings – nearly 10 % of the Austrian export" (Rathkolb, 2010, 905).

To continue this success, the management diversified between 1975 and 1985 its performance in worldwide activities, but ran into a deficit of 285 million Euro (Rathkolb, 2010, 886), primarily due to labor costs. The owner of the company (the state), in cooperation with the works council, did not allow a reduction of the labor force, and the managers tried to add several branches outside of steel production. With this deficit the top manager was fired in 1985 (Rathkolb, 2010, 916) and replaced with several top managers in the following years to start the fight to save the company. Finally, the workforce could be reduced, but the surplus of workers was transferred into a "steel foundation," where they found training for new jobs and were financially supported. In total the adjustments were done in the area of quality requirements but based on acceptance rules. The result was positive, the company was completely privatized, and the solution included share holdings of two local banks, and approximately 11 % of the shares were owned by an employee fund (Stelzer, 2010, 35). With this base and the quality of leadership the company grew to a highly successful international organization. In 2010 it had 41,018 employees with 51 % working in international locations and only 49 % in Austria.

The ups and downs of banks and a steel company in Austria demonstrate only three instances of the Austrian economy and its social developments. "Like each societal institution, also the economic partnership is subject to new challenges and changes of structures. The functioning system of the economic partnership gives Austria without doubts an international advantage of location, which is in the face of increasing internationalization of the economy of increasing importance for the country" (Novotny, 1991, 305). In the terms of North, the Austrian participation system integrated completely the institutional level with the organizational level.

2 Czech Republic

Immediately after the countries in Middle and Eastern Europe were liberated in 1989, the Johannes Kepler University tried to get in contact with universities in these countries and partnership agreements were signed, in the Czech Republic with the University of Law and the University of Economics among others. Especially the contact with the University of Economics became very active step by step, including four US/Canadian universities. The visit of Prof. Keim from Texas A&M University intensified the cooperation. He organized a US stipend for an executive teaching program, in which JKU also got involved. The program led to the foundation of an executive program at the University of Economics in Prague (PIBS – Prague International Business School) under the leadership of Prof. Maly. This school provided us the opportunity to teach the Vroom/Yetton model in Prague, Ceske Budjovice, Brno, and Olomouc, and provided us the Czech data between 1991 and 2015 and gave us the chance of interaction with colleagues at the University of Economics and the executives in the training programs. Reber et al. (2004) were able to compare the behavior of Austrian and Czech managers for the first time.

The contacts with the executives provided a good picture of the Czech effort to transfer the state ownership to all citizens based on a voucher system, as well as national and international firms (Kost, 1994, 122–152; Piske, 2004). One takeover attracted special attention: the takeover of Skoda by Volkswagen

(Dorow & Varga von Kibed, 1997). The process of integration was to be done as quickly as possible, the involved managers of both nationalities were ill prepared for this task, and essential conflicts between the Czech and the German (expatriates) were expected. In order to overcome these conflicts, a special organizational structure in the form of a matrix, called a tandem system, was introduced. For the most important hierarchical positions, from the members of the managing board down through the hierarchy, a German and a Czech manager had the same formal power. Only upon agreement by each of the two partners could a decision be considered as rendered. In the beginning the "Tandem" was a challenging mission accompanied by numerous conflicts, but the decisions had to be made in order to make the new Skoda successful. This was achieved despite the high labor costs for the German and also the Czech employees. The integration process had become successful, the partners had learned to trust each other and learned to cooperate. In this stage we could apply the Vroom/Yetton model, and the integration showed us a unique result: Auer-Rizzi and Reber (2013) could show that the mean level of participation of Skoda managers (MLP = 4.90) was in the middle between "other" Czech managers (MLP = 4.30) and German (MLP = 5.35) managers and that the Skoda managers are significantly different from the "other" Czech managers (p. 23). This example shows in the model of North the impact of learning and change completely on a company level.

3 (West-)Germany

For Germany the question of how to survive and recover, and what strategy could help them out of the disaster was capitalism versus social partnership. The answer was the latter, but in a different form called "Mitbestimmung," translated as "Codetermination," especially on North's level of organizations (companies): The start was the "Montan Mitbestimmungsgesetz" ("Montan Codetermination") for all companies in the area of mining (especially coal), iron and steel – very important companies for the arms industry that had been nationalized.

The reorganization was built on a concept of partnership that was discussed in the literature, but not applied before (Wächter, 1983) – a concept that relates to our discussion of "quality" and "participativeness," and was called "parity codetermination." It is based on a two-tier structure of companies with the advisory board and the managing board. The advisory board included a parity of 50 % on the capital side and 50 % on the labor side, and one neutral member elected by both sides in order to solve a stalemate situation. In the management board, one member was made responsible for personnel and social issues, who

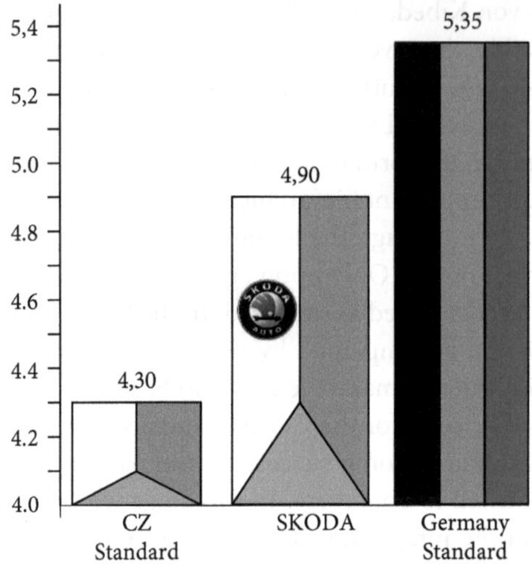

Fig. 1: Mean Level of Participation of Skoda managers in comparison to other Czech and German managers. (Source: Auer-Rizzi & Reber, 2013, 23)

could not be selected against the votes of the labor side. This position is called "Arbeitsdirektor" ("labor director").

This organizational structure was supported by the Western allies – especially by the French foreign minister Robert Schuhman as a concept for Europe (Urwein, 2003, 13), and was accepted by the West German parliament in 1951 (Henssler, 2002, X). When the German parliament became independent, the "Montan"-law was transferred after many discussions to the codetermination law in 1976 for all capital companies with more than 2,000 employees. It also contains the same structure with the same number of seats in the advisory board, but some corrections for the reduction of the representation of labor force: the additional neutral member of the advisory board was appointed by the chairman, who most of the time came from the capital side, and the "labor director" in the management board could be appointed by the capital side alone (Wächter, 1983, 35). No changes were made within the structure of the labor side in the labor committees, for the white- and blue-collar workers were related to the size of the companies, beginning with one person when the company had 20 employees and, for example, 35, when the company would have 7,001 to 9,000 employees (Henssler, 2003, 305 ff).

As for the codetermination on the supranational level, the development started with the first steps of the WEU/EU in 1951 with the treaty in Paris, and 1957 in Rome. But from the start the social policy competencies remained largely a national affaire (Cini, 2002). In all treaties some steps were taken, but the EU's social dimensions could not be harmonized, "... potentially induced by the increased competitive pressures of the single market and Economic and Monetary Union (sometimes called social dumping) ... and the enlargement of the EU will make the adaptation of common standards more difficult" (Falkner, 2002, 276). These predictions became true and only Austria and Germany continued their national partnership structures with the consequences that in Austria and Germany the participative partnership approach declined (Auer-Rizzi et al., 2005; Matzig, 2005; Bickenbach & Soltwedel, 1996).

4 Poland

The data collection in Poland brings into open very unique characteristics. The application of the Vroom/Yetton model was started before the solidarity movement and its victory in 1989, and continued into the time of reconstruction of the state and its economy. As we can see in Tab. 1, the Polish managers demonstrate high violation rates of the acceptance rules from the beginning before the revolution. They are only more participative as the importance of the problems decline (Maczynski, Jago, Reber, & Böhnisch, 1994). This tendency continues after the revolution (Jago, Maczynski, & Reber, 1996; Reber et al., 2004), and in a study based on the GLOBE project, Maczynski et al. (2010, 131) state that "... Polish managers of 2008/2009 have a considerably less negative attitude towards autocratic behavior than their counterparts investigated during 1996/1997. Our research results point to the conclusion that the introduction of a market economy in Poland has shown little effects so far on the leadership behavior of Polish managers."

Maczynski et al. (1997) used the Vroom/Yetton model for a training program in 1997, resulting in the data clearly indicating "... that autocratic leadership styles (AI, AII) decreased substantially and, at the same time, the willingness to include subordinates in the decision-making process increased; ... The result of our research suggest the effective management is a skill possible to be acquired and that it can be learned through instruction by the use of the Vroom/Yetton (1973) and Vroom/Jago (1988) model" (Maczynski, Kwiatkowski, & Arcimowicz, 1997, 333). In contrast to the training effect, the development of the leadership style of the Polish managers also did not follow this tendency after the country entered the EU. This step, together with all the other Middle and East European countries, did not move the economy in the direction of social partnership – their ideals and success are more accomplished in the establishment of an intentionally competitive liberal market economy.

IV Conclusion

The development of Europe was overshadowed by two world wars and four ideologies – imperialism, nationalism, liberalism, communism – as well as an intense learning process. Austria, the "poorest country after the second world war," shied away from all of these ideologies and formed a new one. Together with external help Austria reconstructed the whole state on all levels – individuals, groups, organizations, the constitution of the state – with the principle of social partnership and learned that the quality of decisions in all technical dimensions is also necessary for success. Germany got also support by the European Allies in the reconstruction of its economy. After the First World War, France occupied the German industry in the Ruhr valley, because Germany could not pay reparations. After the Second World War, France supported the reconstruction of the coal, steel, and mining industry with the partnership model of "codetermination," a pattern which Germany later transformed for all larger companies. The Treaty of Rome established the European Economic Community (EEC) and the European Atomic Energy Union (EURATOM – on January 1, 1958 (Urwin, 2002)) as a start of the European Union, which continued to grow. Already before the EU the first steps toward cooperation were underway with the founding of NATO in 1949. Both institutions operated independently at all times, but informally their cooperation was very important during the "cold war," and also after the collapse of the Soviet Union. A marvel occurred, when on October 2, 1990, Germany was liberated (Zelikow & Ricek, 1995), and as a consequence West and East European countries became members of the EU in 1991. Thereby a unique and important partnership was created, but with an emphasis almost solely on political and economic matters, neglecting the "social" side of the partnership (Falkner, 2002; Smith, 2002).

The Vroom/Yetton model, with its simple formula: leadership effectiveness is a function of quality multiplied by acceptance, is helpful for the application of social partnerships. We see in the four countries in the European environment that the quality-function is materialized, but the participative dimension would require learning. In the context of the unification of Europe, particularly the Bologna Agreement stimulated students in Europe to learn and be educated at foreign universities, especially within Europe. This seems to be a great chance in the area of "social partnership." The existing universities are in a national environment and the EU is concentrated on political and economic matters. Where can we find a European investment in the field of education? One example exists in the "European University Viadrina," established in Frankfurt directly on the river Oder, an important river border between the reunited Germany and liberated Poland. The university teaches economics, management, social sciences, and languages, and can survive with the limited funding provided by the German province Brandenburg and Poland. Funding such universities would be an important mission for a social partnership in Europe. The Vroom/Yetton model could help to support effective leadership with many concepts in the social sciences, for example, with the suggestions by "game theories" to establish cooperation.

References

Agar, M. H. (1996): *The professional stranger: An informal introduction to ethnography*. 2nd ed., San Diego: Academic Press.

Auer-Rizzi, W., Reber, G. (2007): Zusammenhang zwischen Corporate Governance Strukturen und Führungsverhalten - Empirische Befunde und Erklärungsansätze. In: U. Jürgens, D. Sadowski, G. F. Schuppert, M. Weiss (Eds.): Perspektiven der Corporate Governance (pp. 182–206). Baden-Baden: Nomos.

Auer-Rizzi, W., Reber, G. (2013): Leadership styles: Intertia and changes in the Czech Republic. *Journal of East European Management Studies*, 18(1), 9–35.

Auer-Rizzi, W., Reber, G., Szabo, E. (2005): Governance-Strukturen und Führungsverhalten: Symptome von Entsolidarisierung in Deutschland und Österreich. *Industrielle Beziehungen*, 12(3): 231–251.

Austrian Parliament (1989): *Parliamentary Administration*. Vienna: The Austrian Parliament.

Bickenbach, F., Soltwedel, R. (1996): *Freiräume schaffen, Motivation stärken, Partizipation fördern: Bausteine partizipativer Führung und Unternehmensorganisation*. Gütersloh: Verlag Bertelsmann Stiftung.

Böhnisch, W. (1991): *Führung und Führungskräftetraining nach dem Vroom/ Yetton Modell*. Stuttgart: Schaeffer-Poeschel.

Bond, M. H. (1992): The process of enhancing cross-cultural competence in Hong-Kong organizations. *International Journal of Intercultural Relations*, 16(4), 395–412.

Chhokar, J. S., Brodbeck, F. C., House, R. J. (2007) (Eds.). *Culture and leadership across the world: The GLOBE book of in-depth studies of 25 societies*. Mahwah: Lawrence Earlbaum Associates.

Cini, M., Pérez-Solórzano Borragán N. (2019) (Eds.). *European Union politics*. Oxford: Oxford University Press.

Coch, L., French, J. R. P. (1948): Overcoming resistance to change. *Human Relations*, 1(4), 512–532.

Dorow, W., Kibed, G. (1997): Market entry in eastern Europe as a challenge for expatriates – case study: The Volkswagen-Skoda joint venture in the Czech Republic. In: D. Wagner (Ed.): Bewältigung des ökonomischen Wandels (pp. 208–216). München: Mering.

Falkner, G. (2002): The EU's social dimension. In: M. Cini (Ed.): *European Union politics* (pp. 264–277). Oxford: Oxford University Press.

French, J. R. P., Isreal, J., As, D. (1960): An experiment on participation in a Norwegian factory. *Human Relations*, 13(1), 3–19.

Henssler, M. (2003): *Mitbestimmungsgesetze*. 7th ed., München: Deutscher Taschenbuch Verlag.

Hofstede, G. (1980): *Culture's consequences: International differences in work-related values*. Beverly Hills: Sage Publications.

Hofstede, G. (2001): *Culture's consequences: Comparing values, behaviors, institutions, and organizations across nations*. 2nd ed., Thousand Oaks: Sage Publications.

Hofstede, G. (2006): What did GLOBE really measure? Researchers' minds versus respondents' minds. *Journal of International Business Studies*, 37(6): 882–896.

House, R. J., Hanges, P., Javidan, M., Dorfmann, P. W., Gupta, V. (2004) (Eds.). *Culture, leadership, and organizations: The GLOBE study of 62 societies*. Thousand Oaks: Sage.

Jago, A. G., Maczynski, J., Reber, G. (1996): Evolving leadership styles? A comparison of Polish managers before and after market economy reforms. *Polish Psychological Bulletin*, 27(2): 107–115.

Jago, A. G., Reber, G., Böhnisch, W. (1986): *Power distance. Predictions of Austrian, Mexican, and US Leadership Styles*. Paper presented at the 18. Annual Meeting of the Decision Science Institute, Honolulu.

Javidan, M., House, R. J., Dorfman, P. W., Hanges, P. J., deLuque, M. S. (2006): Conceptualizing and measuring cultures and their consequences: A comparative review of GLOBE's and Hofstede's approaches. *Journal of International Business Studies*, 37(6): 897–914.

Kahneman, D. (2003): Maps of bounded rationality: A perspective of intuitive judgement and choice. In: T. Frängsmyr (Ed.): *The Nobel Prizes 2002* (pp. 449–477). Stockholm: Nobel Foundation, (https://www.nobelprize.org/nobel_prizes/economic-sciences/laureates/2002/kahnemann-lecture.pdf).

Katz, D., MacCoby, N., Morse, N. C. (1950): *Productivity, supervision, and morale in an office situation*. Ann Abor: University of Michigan Press.

Kost, M. (1994): *Analyse der Industrieprivatisierung in Polen, Ungarn und der CSFR*. Frankfurt a. Main: Peter Lang.

Maczynski, J., Kwiatkowski, P., Arcimowicz, A. (1997): Changing leadership style through training in participative decision making: Application to managerial practices in Polish organizations. *Polish Psychological Bulletin*, 28(4), 333–341.

Maczynski, J., Jago, A. G., Reber, G., Böhnisch, W. (1993): Leadership style of Polish, Austrian, and U.S. managers. *The Review of Psychology*, 1, 65–80.

Maczynski, J., Jago, A. G., Reber, G., Böhnisch, W. (1994): Culture and leadership styles: A comparison of Polish, Austrian, and U.S. managers. *Polish Psychological Bulletin*, 25(4), 303–315.

Maczynski, J., Lobodzinski, A., Wyspianski, D., Kwiatkowski, P. (2010): Differences in organizational practices and preferred leader attributes between Polish managers investigated in 1996/1997 and 2008/2009. *Polish Psychological Bulletin*, 41(4), 127–132.

Maier, N. R. F. (1963): *Problem-solving discussions and conferences: Leadership methods and skills*. New York: McGraw Hill.

Matzig, G. (2005) (Ed.). *Der grosse Graben: Das Ende der Konsensgesellschaft*. München: Süddeutsche Zeitung GmbH.

Miller, K. I., Monge, P. R. (1986): Participation, satisfaction and productivity: A meta-analytic review. *Academy of Management Journal*, 29(4), 727–753.

North, D. C. (1990): *Institutions, institutional change and economic performance*. Cambridge: Cambridge University Press.

North, D. C. (1996): *Institutions, Organizations, and Market Competition*. Working paper, Washington University, St Louis, URL: http://econwpa.repec.org/eps/eh/papers/9612/9612005.pdf (EconWPA, download March 17, 2018).

Nowotny, E. (1991): Wirtschafts- und Sozialpartnerschaft in Österreich – Gesamtwirtschaftliche und einzelbetriebliche Formen und Effekte. *Die Betriebswirtschaft*, 51(3), 287–308.

Piske, R. (2004): *Erfolg deutscher Akquisitionen in Osteuropa: die Rolle von Integrationsmanagement und Kooperationsqualität*. Wiesbaden: Deutscher Universitäts-Verlag.

Preinfalk, H. (2010): Aspects of social partnership in Austria. *WISO*, 33 (Sonderheft), 5–19.

Rathkolb, O. (2010): Mythos VÖEST. In: F. Mayrhofer, W. Schuster (Eds.): *Linz im 20. Jahrhundert: Beiträge, Band 2* (pp. 885–926). Linz: Archiv der Stadt Linz.

Reber, G., Szabo, E. (2007): Culture and leadership in Austria. In: J. S. Chhokar, F. C. Brodbeck, R. J. House (Eds.): *Culture and leadership across the world: The GLOBE book of in-depth studies of 25 societies* (pp. 109–146). Mahwah: Lawrence Earlbaum Associates.

Reber, G., Auer-Rizzi, W., Maly, M. (2004): The behaviour of managers in Austria and the Czech Republic: An intercultural comparison based on the Vroom/Yetton Model of leadership and decision making. *Journal of East European Management Studies*, 9(4), 411–429.

Simon, H. A. (1990): Invariance of human behavior. *Annual Review of Psychology*, 41, 1–19.

Smith, K. E. (2002): EU external relations. In: M. Cini, (Ed.): *European Union politics* (pp. 229–245). Oxford: Oxford University Press.

Smith, P. B. (2006): When elephants fight, the grass gets trampled: The GLOBE and Hofstede projects. *Journal of International Business Studies*, 37(6), 916–921.

Smith, P. B., Peterson, M. F. (1988): *Leadership, organizations and culture*. London, Newbury Park: Sage.

Smith, P. B., Peterson, M. F., and 13 co-authors (1994): Organizational event management in fourteen countries: A comparison with Hofstede's dimensions. In: A.-M. Bouvy, F. J. R. van de Vijver, P. Boski, P. Schmitz (Eds.): Journeys into cross-cultural psychology (pp. 364–373). Amsterdam: Swets and Zeitlinger.

Stelzer, M. (2010): Employee shareholding scheme as a strategic ownership: The equity participation model within the voestalpine group. *WISO*, 33(Sonderheft), 35–49.

Szabo, E. (2007): *Participative management and culture: A qualitative and integrative study in five European countries*. Frankfurt a. Main: Peter Lang.

Tannenbaum, R., Schmidt, W. H. (1958): How to choose a leadership pattern. *Harvard Business Review*, 36(2): 95–101.

Taras, V., Rowney, J., Steel, P. (2009): Half a century of measuring culture: Review of approaches, challenges, and limitations based on the analysis of 121 instruments for quantifying culture. *Journal of International Management*, 15(4), 357–373.

Taras, V., Steel, P., Kirkman, B. (2010): Negative practice-value correlations in the GLOBE data: Unexpected findings, questionnaire limitations and research directions. *Journal of International Business Studies*, 41(8), 1330–1338.

Urwin, D. W. (2002): The European community: from 1945 to 1985. In: M., Cini, (Ed.): *European Union politics* (pp. 11–45). Oxford: Oxford University Press.

Vroom, V. H. (1960): *Some personality determinants of the effects of participation*. Englewood Cliffs: Prentice Hall.

Vroom, V. H. (2000): Leadership and the decision-making process. *Organizational Dynamics*, 28(4), 82–94.

Vroom, V. H., Jago, A. G. (1978): On the validity of the Vroom/Yetton model. *Journal of Applied Psychology*, 63(2), 151–162.

Vroom, V. H., Yetton, P. W. (1973): *Leadership and decision making*. Chicago: University of Pittsburgh Press.

Wächter, H. (1983): *Mitbestimmung*. München: Vahlen Verlag.

Łukasz Sułkowski

Academic Leadership in University Mergers

Abstract: The practice of consolidating universities is increasing across the countries, thus the most challenging issue is the role and competencies of academic leaders. Author reviewed theories and concepts of leadership in management and social sciences to highlight the most required competencies of academic leaders which enhance and support the critical and complex processes of mergers and acquisitions in higher education.

Keywords: academic leaders, mergers, acquisitions, higher education, competencies

Introduction

Academic leadership is one of the crucial challenges of university mergers all over the world. Mergers and acquisitions (M&A) is usually a type of radical change that requires transformational leadership to ensure a successful transformation (chapter based on: Sułkowski, 2017a). In this chapter the purpose of academic leadership is to encourage members of the organization to act together, leading to the realization of the goals of the institution of science and higher education. The concepts of academic leadership are derived from a rich theory, developed on the basis of organization, management, psychology, and sociology. The most important research problem concerns effective leadership, which is analyzed from the perspective of various theoretical schools (Ford, Ford, & Polin, 2014).

1 University leadership

The theory of attributes looks for the configuration of personality traits, characteristics of individuals, and competences and skills which are characteristic of an effective leader (Stogdill, 1974). In a university, this favorable configuration of features depends on the type of organization, academic order, and cultural context. The for-profit private university in the English system typically requires leaders resembling the configuration of leaders' features from other service businesses (e.g., consulting, banking), whereas a public university, e.g., in the Scandinavian system, requires a completely different set of features. Research on leadership competencies of academic leaders has been conducted by: J. Yielder, A. Codling, and K. Krintzline (Yielder & Codling, 2004, pp. 315–328; Krintzline, 2016). Concepts based on the theory of traits in academic leadership form the context of some case studies of successful mergers, in which merits are attributed to, among others, traits of leaders (Chetty, 2010; Jansen, 2003, pp. 27–50).

Situational theories seek answers to the question about effective leadership in the management relationship and the conditions for its implementation (Fiedler, 1967). B. Clark's classical power triangle places university management between the influence of the state, the market, and the academic oligarchy (Clark, 2001, pp. 9–24). University leaders and academic managers function in the context of not only the academic order but also: the type of university, social, economic, legal, and cultural conditions. The common features of academic leadership resulting from the essence of a knowledge-oriented organization that combines science with adult education should be: an orientation towards the greater good (science and education), striving for an increase in efficiency, and participative management based on relationships. The concepts of situational academic leadership are used in studies of many universities, as well as in research conducted by, among others, R. Birnbaum and D.D. Warrick (Birnbaum, 1989, pp. 125–136; Warrick, 1981, pp. 155–172).

Management style concepts have been developed for more than half a century. The style of management is the way the manager interacts with the members of the group subordinate to him, perpetuated in his behavior and affecting the group and the results it achieves. The first concepts were created by R. Lippitt and R.K. White and R. Likert (Likert, 1961; 1967), while the most popular concept of management styles is the managerial grid, created in the 1960s by R. Blake and J. Mouton (Blake & Mouton, 1964). Universities belong to organizations that are more often managed using participatory rather than autocratic management styles. A rector's traditional authority is *primus inter pares* in the academic environment, and a knowledge-oriented university organization requires the involvement and cooperation of stakeholders. Management styles of university leaders have been analyzed by many authors: e.g., James S. Pounder, Linda M. Randall, Lori A. Coakley, Eltham Shahmandi (Pounder, 2001, pp. 281–290; Randall & Coakley 2007, pp. 325–335; Shahmandi, 2011, p. 44).

The young but rapidly developing school of leadership is the critical trend that is part of a wider research perspective called Critical Management Studies. The CMS paradigm analyzes the oppressive, unethical, manipulative, and ideological aspects of leadership (Alvesson, & Sveningsson, 2003a, pp. 359–381; Ford, 2005, pp. 236–251; Gedro, 2010, pp. 552–564; Fenwick, 2004, pp. 193–209). The beginnings of critical studies on leadership are associated with the critical analysis of H. Mintzberg's *The Nature of Managerial Work*, conducted by M. Calás and L. Smircich. The authors point to the masculinist model of leadership suggested by Mintzberg (Calás & Smircich, 1991, pp. 567–602). Introspective reflection on academic leadership is developing rapidly and concerns narcissistic leadership, the "glass ceiling", practices and stigmatizing and excluding discourses. The critical trend in research on academic leadership is used by, among others, the founders of the critical trend of H. Willmott and M. Alvesson (Willmott, 1995, pp. 993–1027; Dominici, Fried, & Zeger, 2009, p. 25; Alvesson & Sveningsson, 2003b, pp. 961–988; Khwaja, 2015; Labby, 2010).

The school of neocharismatic and transformation leadership refers to the classical charisma concept of Max Weber (1968) R. House pointed to values' orientation and building trust as distinguishing factors of charismatic leadership leadership (House, 1976) B.M. Bass proposed a distinction between transactional and transformational leadership (Bass, 1999, p. 9–32). Transactional leadership is based on a proposition or promise to exchange symbolic or material goods with a subordinate in return for performing specific tasks. Transformational leadership is about building a new quality of social relations through the joint commitment of the leader and his supporters. A transformational leader aims to change values within the organization, implements his vision, and accomplishes the organization's goals by making involved employees out of the subordinates. Transactional leadership leads to higher efficiency and allows organizations that find themselves in a difficult situation to grow and survive. Neocharismatic and transformational concepts have been used to analyze leadership in universities and are discussed by many authors, including W.F. Brown, D. Moshavi, R.M. Diamond, J.S. Pounder (Brown & Moshavi, 2002, pp. 79–93; Diamond, 2002; Pounder, 2001, pp. 281–290).

The team management school is based on the assumption that the team plays a key leadership role. Worker teams are social groups operating in organizations whose members are entities acting together to achieve common goals. This definition of the staff team reduces leadership to the function of administration, inspiration, and coordination. In 1960, McGrath created a theory of critical control functions, the fulfillment of which is a prerequisite for ensuring the effectiveness of the activities of the worker group without the need to institutionalize the managerial role (Hackman & Walton, 1986, p. 76). G.L. Drecksel said that management means adjusting the team's operations to changing environmental conditions (Drecksel, 1991, pp. 535–546). From this point of view, there is no need to link the process of management with a specific social role. C. Larson and F. LaFasto in 1989 proposed the conditions for the creation of competent, self-directing teams (Larson & LaFasto, 1989). H.P. Sims, Jr. and Ch.C. Manz have developed a theory which can also be included in the mainstream concept of team management (Sims Jr. & Manz, 1996). The authors argue that modern organizations have a horizontal shape, associated with the processes of decentralization and the "slimming down" of the organization; they translate into the creation of worker teams with the authority and scope of responsibility to autonomously manage the group. The concept of team management also includes the concept of leadership substitutes. It is looking for situational factors that replace an effective manager and leader (Kerr & Jermier, 1978, pp. 375–403). In the team management perspective, there are also concepts of bottom-up leadership (Helgesen, 1995). It is a mistake to assign most of the organization's successes to leadership skills of its manager because managers do not become leaders just because of their position. In the organization of the post-capitalist and knowledge-based era, employee teams are the key, not the heads of the organization. The change takes place in the process of distributing power, teams organizing themselves, defining their goals and methods of action, thanks to which they are able to meet the challenges related to the necessity of speedy information processing. The approach of team management and self-leadership is also used in academic leadership in many analyses of the activities of network research teams (Pearce, 2007, pp. 355–359; Bolden, Gosling, & O'Brien, 2012; Gronn, 2002, pp. 423–451; Ball, 2007, pp. 449–477). Some of the described approaches to leadership are also reflected in the research and practice of M&A in enterprises, as well as in mergers between universities.

2 M&A and leadership

In the rich literature on the subject of M&A (Cartwright & Schoenberg, 2006, p. 1), the opinion is often repeated that leadership fulfills a key function during the merger (Sułkowski, 2017b; 2017c). At the same time, the amount of research on the characteristics of effective leadership during the consolidation of enterprises is increasing (Sitkin & Pablo, 2005, pp. 412–422; Junni & Sarala, 2014, pp. 181–200). Paulina Junni and Riikka Mirja Sarala define leadership in consolidation as a control over the activities of members of the organization to achieve common goals during the merger (Junni & Sarala, 2014, pp. 181–200; Yukl, 2012, pp. 66–85). The authors identified 69 publications on leadership research in M&A in the literature on the subject between 2000 and 2013, and conducted an analysis of the frequency of applying different theories to this issue[1].

In M&A research, many leadership concepts developed in the last century in management and organizational theory have been utilized. The most popular

1 P. Junni, R.M. Sarala, op. cit.

approach used in M&A research is the school called "leadership behavior during mergers and acquisitions". The research focuses primarily on effective leadership during the consolidation and:

- The influence of leaders on the results of the merger (Bertoncelj & Kovac, 2007, pp. 167–188),
- The behavior of leaders during the integration process (Bligh, Pearce, & Kohles, 2006, pp. 296–318; Chreim & Tafaghod, 2012, pp. 5–32; Bartels, Pruyn, & de Jong, 2009, pp. 113–128; Froese & Goeritz, 2007, pp. 95–114; Froese, Pak & Chong, 2008, pp. 97–108; Schweiger & Goulet, 2005, pp. 1477–1499),
- Charismatic and transformational leadership in M&A (Chipunza, Samuel & Mariri, 2011, pp. 8337–8346; Hinduan, Wilson-Evered, Moss, & Scannell, 2009, pp. 59–78; Nemanich & Keller, 2007, pp. 49–68; Schweizer & Patzelt, 2012, pp. 298–310),
- Cultural and identity aspects of leadership (Clark, Gioia, Ketchen Jr., & Thomas, 2010, pp. 397–348; Bligh, 2006, pp. 395–426; Drori, Wrzesniewski, & Ellis, 2013, pp. 1717–1741; Kavanagh & Ashkanasy, 2006, pp. 81–103) ,
- Social responsibility, justice, and the ethical perspective of leadership in mergers (Klendauer & Deller, 2009, pp. 29–45; Melkonian, Monin, & Noorderhaven, 2011, pp. 809–837; Meyer, 2001, pp. 47–66; Edwards & Edwards, 2013, pp. 27–54; Barros & Dominguez, 2013, pp. 979–992; Marmenout, 2011, pp. 783–808),
- The characteristics of the leader and communication processes in M&A (Sitkin, Pablo, 2005, pp. 412–422).

A situational approach to leadership in mergers and acquisitions is also quite popular, as it mainly examines the relationship between the effectiveness of management and the terms of the merger. Some studies draw attention to data that suggests that leadership during mergers is more effective if the merger is homogeneous rather than heterogeneous. This means that merging organizations should be similar in certain important respects, such as the business sector, organizational cultures, and cultures of societies[2].

2 G.K., Stahl, C.H. Chua, A.L. Pablo, *Does national context affect target firm employees' trust in acquisitions? A policy-capturing study*, "Management International Review", 2012, 52(3), s. 395–423; F.J. Froese, L.E. Goeritz, op. cit.; C. Gill, *The role of leadership in successful international mergers and acquisitions: Why Renault-Nissan succeeded and Daimlerchrysler-Mitsubishi failed*, "Human Resource Management", 2012, 51(3), s. 433–456.

In recent years, the number of publications falling within the critical trend of M&A leadership has been increasing. Research has been carried out using qualitative methods and mainly concerns:

- Illusions of cognitive and emotional variables affecting leadership in M&A (Sinkovics, Zagelmeyer, & Kusstatscher, 2011, pp. 27–34),
- Discursive, narrative, and critical leadership analyses during the merger (Evans, 2017, pp. 1699–1717; Nokkala &Välimaa, 2017, pp. 225–244),
- Sense making and management of meanings in consolidations (Chreim & Tafaghod, 2012, pp. 5–32),
- Studies on disadvantaged groups in M&A leadership (gender, ethnic groups) (Vaara, 2002, pp. 211–248; 2003, pp. 859–994; Vaara & Monin, 2010, pp. 3–22; Vaara, Sarala, Stahl, & Björkman, 2012, pp. 1–27; Vaara & Tienari, 2011, pp. 370–390).

The theory of leadership traits remains an insufficiently popular approach to M&A. Its theme is the search for traits, competences, and skills of an effective leader in the M&A processes (Bertoncelj & Kovac, 2007, pp. 167–188; Meschi & Metais, 2013, pp. 469–495).

The last and least popular leadership school used in M&A research is the political perspective ("power and politics in mergers"). Research focuses on the legitimacy of the leader's authority, political and diplomatic activities, and on conflicts between stakeholders in M&A(Kavanagh & Ashkanasy, 2006, pp. 81–103; Rees & Edwards, 2009, pp. 24–39; Steensma & Van Milligen, 2003, pp. 113–134).

3 Academic leaders in M&A

G. Harman and K. Harman, in their pioneer publication on the subject of university mergers, noted that "sensitivity to human and cultural factors and effective leadership are the most important factors for achieving success in university merger" (Harman & Harman, 2003, p. 29). It seems that the concepts of leadership most relevant to the subject of university governance are those that relate to the knowledge-based organizations that create them. If we supplement them with leadership in the conditions of radical organizational changes, it seems that four concepts of the leader will be the most appropriate (Georghiou & Cassingena Harper, 2015):

1. Transformational and neocharismatic leadership,
2. The situational school of leadership,
3. Team leadership,
4. The critical perspective of leadership (Sułkowski, 2016).

An important factor from the perspective of merger processes between institutions of higher education is the transformational leadership (Vasilaki, 2011, pp. 394–412) – which is particularly important for a university in the process of radical consolidation and restructuring changes. Firstly, the leader sets the direction of change and allows for quick, efficient, and effective operation. Secondly, it is based on the mutual trust of the leader and team members. Thirdly, the transformational approach is based on values and shaping of collective and individual identities. The relationship of a transformational leader with employees consists of transforming the perception and interpretation of reality (sense making and sense giving), which allows the group to believe in the sense and value of the change that is taking place. At the same time, as research on leadership in M&A shows, this "management of meanings" can instigate the danger of creating illusions and making mistakes (Vaara, 2003, pp. 859–894; Yu, Engleman, & Van de Ven, 2005, pp. 1501–1528). Therefore, the perspective of transformational leadership should be balanced, and its task is to combine a positive attitude to change with a pragmatic view of the process of its implementation.

The situational school of leadership is a broad umbrella, under which there are diverse concepts of leadership and academic management, combined with the idea of changeability and the contingency of organizational processes. The basis of the research is searching for the conditions of effective leadership in university merger processes (Ahmadvand, Heidari, Hosseini, & Majdzadeh, 2012, p. 736). The conditions of the success of mergers and effective leadership during the consolidation are numerous, which means there exists a need to analyze them as individual cases and then to compare them. In the literature on the subject of university mergers, case studies are the most numerous, although at the same time comparative analysis is lacking. In the induction process, we gather more and more data on effective leadership, for which it is currently difficult to build a universal theory. Among many variables impacting effective leadership appearing in university mergers, the following can be mentioned:

- Type of university,
- Type of merger,
- Purpose of the merger[3],
- Resources involved,

3 J. Martin, *Merging Colleges for Mutual Growth. A New Strategy for Academic Managers*, Johns Hopkins University Press, 1994.

- Organizational cultures and cultural context,
- Organizational strategies,
- Organizational structures,
- Relations between stakeholders,
- Influence of central government,
- Traits and competences of leaders and managers,
- Dynamics of the merger process (Locke, 2007, pp. 83–102)..

Team leadership in complex organizations such as universities plays a key role. The dynamics of consolidation processes additionally increases the level of uncertainty and risk in leadership activities. Effective consolidations of universities can only be carried out by committed, competent, and flexible employee teams. The role of leaders is important because it involves making strategic decisions, but with such a high level of organizational complexity in merger processes, the co-decision makers are mostly team members. Team leadership focuses on self-learning teams that – by cooperating with each other and the environment – develop a consolidation project.

The critical perspective of leadership can be metaphorically compared to a mirror into which academic leaders in the merger processes look. Such a look at one's reflection, sometimes in a distorted mirror, allows you to protect yourself against organizational cynicism (Sloterdijk, 2008) and the instrumental treatment of people over whom you exercise your power. The processes of mergers at universities create changes that may have a negative impact on the subjectivity of people in organizations. The leader may fall into the traps of autocracy, narcissism, oppressive treatment of employees, manipulation of people, and treating the scientific and didactic mission as a smokescreen. Also the very process of a university merger can be treated critically from a radical perspective. It is worth asking whether university consolidations are not a manifestation of fashion, the expansion of new public management, and the development of neo-liberal ideology (Ursin, Aittola, Henderson, & Välimaa, 2010, pp. 327–340). Critical analysis allows leaders to combine ethical solutions with pragmatism necessary to implement organizational changes (Aasen & Stensaker, 2007, pp. 371–383).

References

Alvesson, M., Sveningsson, S. (2003). Good visions, bad micro-management and ugly ambiguity: contradictions of (non-) leadership in a knowledge-intensive organization. *Organization Studies*, 24.6, 961–988.

Alvesson, M., Sveningsson, S. (2003). The great disappearing act: difficulties in doing "leadership". *The Leadership Quarterly*, 14.3, 359–381.

Ball, S. (2007). Leadership of academics in research. *Educational Management Administration & Leadership*, 35.4, 449–477.

Barros, R.H., Dominguez, I.L. (2013). Integration strategies for the success of mergers and acquisitions in financial services companies. *Journal of Business Economics and Management*, 14.5, 979–992.

Bartels, J., Pruyn, A., de Jong, M. (2009). Employee identification before and after an internal merger: A longitudinal analysis. *Journal of Occupational and Organizational Psychology*, 82.1, 113–128.

Bass, B.M. (1999). Two decades of research and development in transformational leadership. *European Journal of Work and Organizational Psychology*, 8.1, 9–32.

Bertoncelj, A., Kovac, D. (2007). An integrated approach for a higher success rate in mergers and acquisitions. *Zbornik Radova Ekonomskog Fakulteta u Rijeci*, 25.3, 167–188.

Birnbaum, R. (1989). The implicit leadership theories of college and university presidents. *The Review of Higher Education*, 12.2, 125–136.

Blake, R.R., Mouton, J.S. (1964). *The managerial grid*. Houston, TX: Gulf.

Bligh, M.C. (2006). Surviving post-merger "culture clash": Can cultural leadership lessen the casualties?. *Leadership*, 2.4, 395–426.

Bligh, M.C., Pearce, C.L., Kohles, J.C. (2006). The importance of self- and shared leadership in team based knowledge work: A meso-level model of leadership dynamics. *Journal of Managerial Psychology*, 21.4, 296–318.

Bolden, R., Gosling, J., O'Brien, A. (2012). *Academic leadership: Changing conceptions, identities and experiences in UK higher education*. Project Report. Exeter: Leadership Foundation for Higher Education.

Brown, W.F., Moshavi, D. (2002). Herding academic cats: Faculty reactions to transformational and contingent reward leadership by department chairs. *Journal of Leadership Studies*, 8.3, 79–93.

Calás, M., Smircich, L. (1991). Voicing Seduction to Silence Leadership. *Organization Studies*, 12.4, 567–602.

Cartwright, S., Schoenberg, R. (2006). Thirty years of mergers and acquisitions research: Recent advances and future opportunities. *British Journal of Management*, 17, 1.

Chetty, G. (2010). *The transformation of the South African higher education sector through mergers-the case study of the Durban University of Technology*. PhD Thesis.

Chipunza, C., Samuel, M.O., Mariri, T. (2011). Leadership style, employee motivation and commitment: Empirical evidence from a consolidated retail bank operating in a depressed economy. *African Journal of Business Management*, 5.20, 8337–8346.

Chreim, S., Tafaghod, M. (2012). Contradiction and Sensemaking in Acquisition Integration. *The Journal of Applied Behavioral Science*, 48.1, 5–32.

Clark, B. (2001). The entrepreneurial university: New foundations for collegiality, autonomy, and achievement. *Higher Education Management*, 13.2.

Clark, S.M., Gioia, D.A., Ketchen Jr., D.J., Thomas, J.B. (2010). Transitional identity as a facilitator of organizational identity change during a merger. *Administrative Science Quarterly*, 55.3, 397–438.

Diamond, R.M. (2002). *Field Guide to Academic Leadership: A Publication of the National Academy for Academic Leadership*. Indianapolis: Customer Care Center.

Dominici, F., Fried, L.P., Zeger, S.L. (2009). So few women leaders. *Academe*, 95.4, 25.

Drecksel, G.L. (1991). *Leadership research. Some issues*. In: J.A. Anderson (ed.), *Communication yearbook*, 14, Newbury Park, CA: Sage, 535–546.

Drori, I., Wrzesniewski, A., Ellis, S. (2013). One out of many? Boundary negotiation and identity formation in post-merger integration. *Organization Science*, 24.6, 1717–1741.

Edwards, M.R., Edwards, T. Employee responses to changing aspects of the employer brand following a multinational acquisition: A longitudinal study. *Human Resource Management*, 52.1, 27–54.

Evans, L. (2019). The worst of times? A tale of two higher education institutions in France: their merger and its impact on staff working lives. *Studies in Higher Education*, 42.9.

Nokkala, T., Välimaa, J. (2017). *Finnish mergers: Change in the Context of Continuity*. In: *Policy Analysis of Structural Reforms in Higher Education*. Springer International Publishing, 225–244.

Fenwick, T.J. (2004). Toward a critical HRD in theory and practice. *Adult Education Quarterly*, 54.3, 193–209.

Fiedler, F.E. (1967). *A theory of leadership effectiveness*. New York: McGraw-Hill.

Ford, J. (2005). Examining leadership through critical feminist readings. *Journal of Health Organization and Management*, 19.3, 236–251.

Ford, J.D., Ford L., Polin, B. (2014). Leadership in the conduct of organizational change: An integrative view. *Academy of Management Proceedings*, 1.

Froese, F.J., Goeritz, L.E. (2007). Integration management of western acquisitions in Japan. *Asian Business & Management*, 6.1, 95–114.

Froese, F.J., Pak, Y.S., Chong, L.C. (2008). Managing the human side of cross-border acquisitions in South Korea. *Journal of World Business*, 43.1, 97–108.

Gedro, J. (2010). Lesbian presentations and representations of leadership, and the implications for HRD. *Journal of European Industrial Training*, 34.6, 552–564.

Georghiou, L., Cassingena Harper, J. (2015). *Mergers and alliances in context.* In: A. Curaj, L. Georghiou, J. Casingena Harper, R. Pricopie, E. Egron-Polak (eds.), *Mergers and alliances in higher education: Internal practice and emerging opportunities*, Heidelberg: Springer.

Gill, C. (2012). The role of leadership in successful international mergers and acquisitions: Why Renault–Nissan succeeded and Daimlerchrysler–Mitsubishi failed. *Human Resource Management*, 51.3, 433–456.

Gronn, P. (2002). Distributed leadership as a unit of analysis. *The Leadership Quarterly*, 13.4, 423–451.

Hackman, J.R., Walton, R.E. (1986). *Leading groups in organizations.* In: P.S. Goodman & Associates (eds.), *Designing Effective Work Groups*, San Francisco: Jossey-Bass, 76.

Helgesen, S. (1995). *The Web of Inclusion: A New Architecture for Building Great Organisations.* New York: Currency/Doubleday.

Hinduan, Z.R., Wilson-Evered, E., Moss, S., Scannell, E. (2009). Leadership, work outcomes and openness to change following an Indonesian bank merger. *Asia Pacific Journal of Human Resources*, 47.1, 59–78.

House, R.J. (1976). A 1976 Theory of Charismatic Leadership. *Working Paper Series*, 06.

Jansen, J. (2003). Mergers in South African higher education: Theorising change in transitional contexts. *Politikon*, 30.1, 27–50.

Junni, P., Sarala, R.M. (2014). *The Role of Leadership in Mergers and Acquisitions: A Review of Recent Empirical Studies.* In: S. Finkelstein, C.L. Cooper (eds.), *Advances in Mergers and Acquisitions*, 13, Bingley: Emerald Group Publishing Limited, 181–200.

Kavanagh, M.H., Ashkanasy, N.M. (2006). The impact of leadership and change management strategy on organizational culture and individual acceptance of change during a merger. *British Journal of Management*, 17.S1, 81–103.

Kerr, S., Jermier, J.M. (1978). Substitutes for leadership: Their meaning and measurement. *Organisational Behavior and Human Performance*, December 1978, 375–403.

Khwaja, T. (2015). *The Language of Leadership a Feminist Poststructural Discourse Analysis of Inaugural Addresses by Presidents of High Profile Research Universities.* The College of William and Mary.

Klendauer, R., Deller, J. (2009). Organizational justice and managerial commitment in corporate mergers. *Journal of Managerial Psychology*, 24.1–2, 29–45.

Krintzline, K. (2016). *Examining university administrators' leadership styles and their influence on the sense of belonging of adjunct instructors teaching online courses.* PhD Thesis, Northcentral University.

Labby, S.A. (2010). *The Relationship among Principal's Emotional Intelligence Skills with Respect to School Accountability Ratings and Selected Demographic Factors.* Sam Houston State University.

Larson, C.E., LaFasto, F.M.J. (1989). *Teamwork: What Must Go Right/What Can Go Wrong.* Newbury Park, CA: Sage Publications.

Likert, R. (1961). *New Patterns of Management.* New York: McGraw Hill.

Likert, R. (1967). *The Human Organization: Its Management and Value.* New York: McGraw Hill.

Locke, W. (2007). Higher education mergers: Integrating organisational cultures and developing appropriate management styles. Higher Education Quarterly, 61.1, 83–102.

Marmenout, K. (2011). Peer interaction in mergers: Evidence of collective rumination. *Human Resource Management*, 50.6, (Special Issue), 783–808.

Martin, J. (1994). *Merging Colleges for Mutual Growth. A New Strategy for Academic Managers.* Baltimore, MD: Johns Hopkins University Press.

Melkonian, T., Monin, P., Noorderhaven, N.G. (2011). Distributive justice, procedural justice, exemplarity, and employees' willingness to cooperate in M&A integration process: An analysis of the Air France–KLM merger. *Human Resource Management*, 50.6, 809–837.

Meschi, P.-X., Metais, E. (2013). Do firms forget about their past acquisitions? Evidence from French acquisitions in the United States (1988–2006). *Journal of Management*, 39.2, 469–495.

Meyer, C.B. (2001). Allocation processes in mergers and acquisitions: An organizational justice perspective. *British Journal of Management*, 12.1, 47–66.

Nemanich, L.A., Keller, R.T. (2007). Transformational leadership in an acquisition: A field study of employees. *Leadership Quarterly*, 18.1, 49–68.

Patzelt, H., Schweizer L. (2012). Employee commitment in the post-acquisition integration process: The effect of integration speed and leadership. *Scandinavian Journal of Management*, 28.4, 298–310.

Pearce, C.L. (2007). The future of leadership development: The importance of identity, multi-level approaches, self-leadership, physical fitness, shared leadership, networking, creativity, emotions, spirituality and on-boarding processes. *Human Resource Management Review*, 17.4, 355–359.

Pounder, J.S. (2001). "New leadership" and university organisational effectiveness: exploring the relationship. *Leadership & Organization Development Journal*, 22.6, 281–290.

Randall, L.M., Coakley, L.A. (2007). Applying adaptive leadership to successful change initiatives in academia. *Leadership & Organization Development Journal*, 28.4, 325–335.

Rees, C., Edwards, T. (2009). Management strategy and HR in international mergers: Choice, constraint, and pragmatism. *Human Resource Management Journal*, 19.1, 24–39.

Schweiger, D.M., Goulet, P.K. (2005). Facilitating acquisition integration through deep-level cultural learning interventions: A longitudinal field experiment. *Organization Studies*, 26.10, 1477–1499.

Shahmandi, E. (2011). Competencies, roles and effective academic leadership in world class university. *International Journal of Business Administration*, 2.1, 44.

Sims Jr., H.P., Manz, Ch.C. (1996). *Company of Heroes. Unleashing the Power of Self-Leadership*. New York: John Wiley.

Sinkovics, R.R., Zagelmeyer, S., Kusstatscher, V. (2011). Between merger and syndrome: The intermediary role of emotions in four cross-border M&As. *International Business Review*, 20.1, 27–34.

Sitkin, S.B., Pablo, A. (2005). *The neglected importance of leadership in mergers and acquisitions*. In: G.K. Stahl, M.E. Mendenhall (eds.), *Mergers and acquisitions: Managing culture and human resources*, Stanford, CA: Stanford University Press, 412–422.

Sloterdijk, P. (2008). *Krytyka cynicznego rozumu*. Wrocław: Wydawnictwo Naukowe Dolnośląskiej Szkoły Wyższej.

Stahl, G.K., Chua, C.H., Pablo, A.L. (2012). Does national context affect target firm employees' trust in acquisitions? A policy-capturing study. *Management International Review*, 52.3, 395–423.

Steensma, H., Van Milligen, F. (2003). Bases of power, procedural justice outcomes of mergers: The push and pull factors of influence tactics. *Journal of Collective Negotiations*, 30.2, 113–134.

Stogdill, R. (1974). *Handbook of Leadership: A Survey of Theory and Research*. New York: The Free Press.

Sułkowski, Ł. (2016). *Kultura akademicka: koniec utopii?*. Warszawa: PWN.

Sułkowski, Ł. (2017). "Fuzjomania" akademicka. Czy Polskę czeka fala konsolidacji uniwersytetów?. Nauka i Szkolnictwo Wyższe, 2.50, 173–188.

Sułkowski, Ł. (2017). *Fuzje uczelni – czy w szaleństwie jest metoda?*. Warszawa: PWN.

Sułkowski, Ł. (2017). *University Mergers—Poland on the Background of International Trends. Management in the Time of Networks, Cross-cultural Activities and Flexible Organizations*. Kraków: Kraków University of Economics.

Vaara, E. (2002). On the discursive construction of success/failure in narratives of post-merger integration. *Organization Studies*, 23.2, 211–248.

Vaara, E. (2003). Post-acquisition integration as sensemaking: Glimpses of ambiguity, confusion, hypocrisy, and politicization. *Journal of Management Studies*, 40.4, 859–894.

Vaara, E., Monin, P. A recursive perspective on discursive legitimation and organizational action in mergers and acquisitions. *Organization Science*, 21.1, 3–22.

Vaara, E., Sarala, R., Stahl, G., Björkman, I. (2012). The impact of organizational and national cultural differences on social conflict and knowledge transfer in international acquisitions. *Journal of Management Studies*, 49.1, 1–27.

Vaara, E., Tienari, J. (2011). On the narrative construction of multinational corporations: An antenarrative analysis of legitimation and resistance in a cross-border merger. *Organizational Science*, 22.2, 370–390.

Vasilaki, A. Culture distance and cross-border acquisition performance: The moderating effect of transformational leadership. *European Journal of International Management*, 5.4, 394–412.

Warrick, D.D. (1981). Leadership styles and their consequences. *Journal of Experiential Learning and Simulation*, 3.4, 155–172.

Weber, M. (1968). *On Charisma and Institution Building*. Chicago: University of Chicago Press.

Willmott, H. (1995). Managing the academics: Commodification and control in the development of University Education in the UK. *Human Relations*, 48.9, 993–1027.

Yielder, J., Codling, A. (2004). Management and leadership in the contemporary university. *Journal of Higher Education Policy and Management*, 26.3, 315–328.

Yu, J., Engleman, R.M., Van de Ven, A.H. (2005). The integration journey: An attention-based view of the merger and acquisition integration process. *Organization Studies*, 26.10, 1501–1528.

Yukl, G. (2012). Effective leadership behavior: What we know and what questions need more attention. *Academy of Management Perspectives*, 26.4, 66–85.

Łukasz Haromszeki and Tadeusz Listwan

Organisational Leaders in Public Institutions: Operating Amidst the Prevalent and Desirable Organisational Culture

Abstract: The chapter presents key elements of the organizational culture in public institutions where there are leadership relationships. The research was also conducted to find the answer to question what determines the ideal organizational culture desired by the leaders. The authors indicate problems that labor market experience nowadays and give some predictions for the future.

Keywords: public institutions, organizational culture, leadership relationships, longitudinal study, Office of a Future

1 Introduction

Over the past years, there have been clear changes in the field of work and attitudes towards external stakeholders in the public sector. Before the implemented changes, rational decision-making in the field of human resource management was a marginal phenomenon. People managing public institutions, individual organisational units and their employees did not feel the need to go beyond the basic operating standards set by the law. Public institutions, including local government units, did not react to changes in the environment because the stakeholders were suppliants, and the financing was independent of the quality of management (Haromszeki, 2016). This situation changed after Poland's accession to the structures of the European Union and the appearance of ISO 9001 quality management standards in the country. The new requirements led to a shift away from approaching stakeholders as suppliants, but rather as customers. This resulted in an improvement in the quality of work, but also limited job security. Qualification and competence requirements also increased (Haromszeki, 2014, pp. 81–101). The dynamization of the functioning of public organisations in Poland resulted in the fact that under the new conditions the most effective approach to the employees, consistent with the expected impact, is to lead them.

In light of this, it can be assumed that there were some sociocultural conditions conducive to the formation of leadership relationships. By distinguishing the variables and seeing how they affect leadership attitudes and behaviours, this chapter aims to identify and present important elements of the organisational culture that dominates public institutions in which there are leadership relationships, and to present opinions and ideas about the specifics of future leadership relationships.

Research of organisational cultures preferred by leaders in public institutions was conducted by the PAPI, CATI and CAWI methods, from 2014 to 2016. The chosen way of defining the leadership and organisational culture is presented in the next part of this chapter.

2 Basic concepts and determinants of the leadership relationship in public organisations

An important role in shaping the contemporary definition of leadership has been played by the situational approach, which emphasises the multidirectional relationship between the individual characteristics of the leader and the factors existing in their environment. Of particular value are the studies of R. Tannenbaum and W.H. Schmidt (after Kuc, 2006 p. 397), F. Fiedler (after Koźmiński, W. Piotrowski, 2006, p. 343), M. Evans and R. House, and V. Vroom, P. Yetton and A.G. Yago (after Griffin, 1997, pp. 507–513), G.A. Yukl (1989), B.M. Bass (1990), R.S. Lord, R.J. Foti and C.L. DeVader (1984), J. Zaccaro, R.J. Foti, D.A. Kenny (1991), M.A. Hogg, R. Martin, K. Weeden, O. Epitropaki (2001), M. Kets de Vries (2008) and J.M. Kouzes and B.Z. Posner (2010). The results of situational leadership research correspond with the definition proposed by W.C.H. Prentice, who indicates "leadership means achieving the goal by pointing people in a specific direction. The leader is the one who leads their co-workers day by day to achieve specific goals in widely varied circumstances" (Prentice, 1961).

In Poland, research on leadership was mainly conducted by J. Mączyński, S. Chełpa and T. Listwan, C. Sikorski and A. K. Koźmiński, which resulted in the formulation of definitions of leadership. A team of scientists from various countries around the world, including J. Mączyński, developed a definition of leadership in the GLOBE project in 1994 in Calgary, which stands as follows: "Leadership is the ability of the individual to influence, motivate and enable others to contribute to the success of their organisation," (Hartog, Koopman, Thierry, Wilderom, Mączyński and Jarmuż, 1997, p. 387–413). S. Chełpa and T. Listwan define leadership as a special kind of management based on authority and emotional ties, strongly stimulating employee motivation (Chełpa, 2010, p. 526). C. Sikorski acknowledges "the idea of leadership is related to the concept of transformational management. Changes taking place in the modern world require the involvement of people motivated and prepared to work, based on conscious acceptance of the complexity of the modern social and economic world. In this sense, leadership is about the ability to create a vision that is able to inspire and bring employees with it" (Sikorski, 2006, p. 6). A.K. Koźmiński writes: "Speaking of leadership, we mean an important resource of the organisation, an element of its social potential: the sum of abilities, skills and talents of the influence of some members of the organisation on others, so that it is possible to achieve the goals set by the organization" (Koźmiński, 2004, p. 151).

On the basis of the abovementioned definitions, it is assumed that "organisational leadership is the relationship of the superior with subordinates/co-workers…" (Haromszeki, 2010, pp. 40–41). According to this definition, a leader is a person who not only feels appointed to fulfil this role, but above all is considered a leader by their followers. P. Drucker (2004) took a similar stance. This approach results in a situation where leadership occurs only in real situations of impact on people and can be examined only from a pragmatic perspective, as an explanation of effective action that has ended and has measurable effects (Haromszeki, 2010). Therefore, the conducted research included only people who are considered leaders and achieved successes (organisational goals) with the active participation of their subordinates/co-workers.

The second key term of this chapter is organisational culture. E. Schein (1985) defines organisational culture as "a pattern of basic assumptions – invented, discovered or developed by a given group during the learning process, dealing with the problems of external adaptation and internal integration – functioning well enough to be considered right and appropriate to communicate to new members of the community as an appropriate way of perceiving, feeling and responding to these problems." According to E. Schein, three levels of organisational culture can be distinguished (after Kuc, Moczydłowska, 2009):

- Basic assumptions, constituting the core of the culture, giving the basis for its other components, responding to the problems of the essence of existence, human nature, reality and truth,
- Norms and values, which constitute the observable level of culture more successfully than the basic assumptions, expressed in the views on the attitudes of members of the organisation,
- Artefacts and products, which constitute an observable component and indicator of organisational culture, i.e. material culture of the organisation. They include organisational structure, procedures and systems, and organisational behaviours. Behaviours, rituals and myths are also among cultural indicators at this level.

Organisational culture is an important determinant of the effectiveness of activities. One of the internal functions mentioned by E. Schein is the determination of the principles of power and status criteria. According to E. Schein, it allows one to avoid a number of conflicts over power, many negative emotions and aggressive actions. It defines how authority can be achieved, maintained, used, displayed and referred to. It informs what is allowed and what is forbidden and to what extent it is possible to criticise those in power, and offers a common system of values related to organisational influence (after Kuc, Moczydłowska, 2009).

Significant research in the field of organisational culture was also conducted by K.S. Cameron and R.E. Quinn (2006), where they developed a questionnaire for assessing organisational culture based on a theoretical model – a model of competing values. The authors described four dominant types of culture: hierarchy, market, clan and adhocracy. They also demonstrated the usefulness of the model of competing values for determining organisational schemes, individual organisational life cycles, quality issues, efficiency theories, leadership roles and the role of human resource management (HRM) and managerial skills. Hierarchy culture in this model is characterised by stability and control as well as its focus on internal affairs and integration. On the other hand, market culture is characterised by stability and control as well as its focus on the position in the environment and diversity. Clan culture is characterised by flexibility and freedom of action, and focuses on internal affairs and integration. The most dynamic culture, adhocracy, is characterised by flexibility and freedom of action as well as its focus on the position in the environment and diversity.

New concepts in the field of HRM indicate that organisational cultures change with the increase in employee awareness. The hierarchical organisational structure, with a large distance of power, gives way to a greater understanding of the needs of employees, and inspires them to show initiative in order to improve their work from the bottom up (Listwan, ed. 2010, Sikorski, 2006). In this understanding of organisational reality, one would assume that in various types of organisations (including public ones) we are dealing with a phenomenon described by E. Fromm, according to whom emancipation of employees can change their relations with superiors. Fromm described a concrete difference between the *rational authority* – having its source in competences, temporariness, dependence on conditions in a given place and time – and the *irrational authority* – imposed and uncritical, showing relations of inequalities between the manager and the employees (Fromm, 1947). One should consider whether the above-defined types of authorities are mutually exclusive or if, for example, public institutions (especially the studied local government units) are the place where irrational and rational elements are combined. It also seems unlikely that Fromm's sense of freedom characterises organisational leaders and their subordinates/co-workers employed in public institutions in Poland. In these organisations such a significant modification of organisational culture, in order to facilitate the release of the potential of employees over the next few years, also seems rather unlikely. Opinions of organisational leaders in this area obtained in the research conducted between 2014 and 2016 are presented later in this chapter.

The multi-spatial perspective of organisational leadership in public institutions is complemented by the results obtained in the previously conducted surveys of employees' opinions on the preferred nature of their relationship with the leader and the characteristics, attitudes and behaviours expected from the leader (Haromszeki, 2014). The research shows that the organisational leader should: be an authority in their field, a professional; have above-average communication skills and good contact with various stakeholders, as well as be a moral authority, and an honest and trustworthy person (Haromszeki, 2014). Expectations of ideal supervisors, though seemingly point to the characteristics of the rational leadership relationship and are a model set of attributes, are not detached from the existing reality.

In the longitudinal study (interviews and observations) – conducted during the project entitled"Leaders and activities of local communities in 2006–2016" (Haromszeki, 2016), it appears that employees of public organisations need leaders who easily adapt to their position, and who easily accept responsibility for their work and their subordinates. These studies in local government offices in Poland suggest that if there is a change in attitudes and behaviours as part of leadership relationships in public organisations, it will be the result of revolutionary modernisation in terms of legal, political, economic, market and socio-cultural conditions (including explicitly articulated employee expectations). The problem in the process of implementing these changes may turn out to be the leaders themselves, who feel the most comfortable within the current shape of the organisation – with the dominant hierarchy and the clear determination of tasks and responsibilities in an autocratic style. The reluctance to change may also stem from the fact that the majority of employees in public institutions accept the current nature of their relations with superiors (Haromszeki, 2016). So far, various studies conducted in the field of leadership give ground to believe that the concept of self-leadership developed by P. Sims and Ch.C. Manz (1996) may not apply to public institutions, not only now but also in the future.

The reason for the inability to observe such a phenomenon is the attitudes and expectations of employees of these institutions, including those employed in local government units (municipal offices). Thus the role of the organisational leader, as assumed in the context of the research conducted and repeatedly mentioned in this chapter, will not rely on preparing employees to undertake the role of operational leaders or withdrawing from making current decisions and controlling every activity of the subordinates (Sikorski, 2006). The growing importance of delegating privileges and the decentralisation of power means that conditions for implementing a democratic style of leadership in public organisations would begin to appear. This phenomenon is unlikely in public institutions in the near future, because even in the business sector the popularity of the autocratic style is growing (Mączyński, Wyspiański, 2011). Research on the leadership styles of organisational leaders (Haromszeki, 2017) also indicates that in both public and private organisations, leaders prefer a negotiating style to flexibly adapt their qualifications and capabilities to existing expectations and internal and external conditions. Using this approach, they ensure an adequate level of employee satisfaction without making significant cultural and organisational changes. The characteristics of research conducted in public organisations, the results of which form the core of this chapter, are presented in the next section.

3 Characteristics of research conducted in public organisations

The aim of the research presented in this chapter is to diagnose the type of organisational cultures in public organisations where leadership relationships exist, and to determine the ideal organisational culture desired by the leaders, which could be used in the organisation within the next five years.

Determination of the purpose of the study, as well as verification and falsification of the initial assumptions during the pilot studies, allowed the authors to formulate the following research problems in the form of questions:

- What type of organizational culture exists in the organisation?
- What are the expectations of organisational leaders regarding the desired future organisational culture, and do they coincide with the concepts of future employee expectations proposed in the literature of this field?
- Is a sense of freedom important for organisational leaders?

The results were compared in terms of the "sense of freedom" with the current assessment, and indicate the desired organisational culture – because the sense of freedom is an important part of the process of shaping the leadership relationship within organisational cultures. For example, in the case of the culture of adhocracy, unlimited freedom is the basis for effective action. In the culture of hierarchy, however, limited freedom is an immanent part of the subordination and legitimisation of the existing power structure.

Questionnaires were conducted in Poland from November 2014 to October 2016. The research population, which was intentionally selected, was made up of successful organisational leaders (measurable results of leadership) as an outcome of their influence on subordinates and with their participation. As a result of this approach, multi-range questionnaire interviews were conducted with 92 organisational leaders in public institutions (local government units).

The selection of a purposive sample relied on the application of two basic criteria:

1. Recognition of a person as a leader by subordinates,
2. Achieving real leadership successes, i.e. achieving goals with the active participation of subordinates and co-workers.

The study employed indirect measurement methods (PAPI, CATI, CAWI). For the purpose of research, Cameron and Quinn's questionnaire was used, among others, for the evaluation of organisational culture, as well as an original questionnaire for the study of organisational leaders (the part concerning personal freedom).

Cameron and Quinn's Organisational Culture Assessment Instrument (OCAI) is a questionnaire that requires answers to six questions. Its goal in the first stage of the proceedings is to help determine the current type of organisational culture. The second stage allows for the specification of the type of organisational culture that the employees think should be implemented in order for the company to succeed in the future. The same questionnaire is completed twice, in the manner described above. The aim of the questionnaire is to define six basic dimensions of the described organisational culture. The results obtained are different for each organisation because they refer to the actual and desired status reported by the employees participating in the survey. Questions used in the questionnaire relate to the evaluation of the organisation's work. For each of the six questions, four answers were given, between which 100 points should be divided, depending on the extent to which the given answer reflects the situation in the respondent's organisation. The results established are the mathematical sum of each of the four categories describing a different type of culture.

The types of culture included in the questionnaire are as follows:

A. Clan culture – *a very friendly workplace where people are willing to interact with one another, similar to a large family. Bosses and superiors take on the role of advisers, teachers or even parents. The organisation prevails thanks to the loyalty of the employees and the attachment to tradition. A high degree of involvement is observed, and the organisation emphasizes the long-term benefits of personal development, attaching great importance to cohesion and morale. The measure of success is the development of human resources and care for employees. The organisation highly values teamwork, participation and consensus.*

B. Culture of adhocracy – *the organisation is dominated by dynamics, entrepreneurship and creativity. People are not afraid of risk, and leaders are considered innovators and visionaries. Assuring the cohesion of the organisation is the desire to experiment and introduce new products. It is important to take the lead in one's field. In the long-term, the organisation focuses on growth, undertaking challenges and acquiring new resources. The measure of success is the possibility to offer unique and new products or services. The position of a leader in the field of products or services is being sought. The organisation encourages freedom and initiative.*
C. Market culture – *for the organisation, results are paramount, while the main concern is the implementation of tasks. People are very ambitious and aim to achieve goals. The leader is a supervisor focused on competitiveness and production. They are ruthless and demanding. The cohesion of the organisation is ensured by expansiveness and the desire to win. The main concern is reputation and success. Competitiveness and achieving measurable goals are what counts in the long run, and the measure of success is market share and market penetration. Competitive prices and market leadership are important, and the management style is to promote strong competition.*
D. Hierarchy culture – *a highly formalised workplace in which a strict hierarchy is in force, where everything is controlled by procedure. Leaders pride themselves on being good coordinators and organisers focused on efficiency. Of greatest importance is the efficient functioning of the organisation. Consistency is provided by formal rules and regulations. In the long term, it is about stability, performance and work without interruption. The measures of success are: reliability of deliveries, keeping schedules, and low costs. Employee management focuses on employment security, ensuring stability and predictability* (Cameron and Quinn, 2006, p. 62).

One question from the original questionnaire in the study of organisational leaders regarding their assessment of personal freedom was also selected for analysis.

Respondents had four possible answers to choose from.

- I definitely feel free,
- I mostly feel free,
- I do not feel free,
- I definitely do not feel free.

The results were subjected to a descriptive analysis, and the relationship between variables was determined using the Kruskal-Wallis test and the Mann-Whitney U test. The results of the analysis are presented in the next part of this chapter.

4 Research results

As a result of the analysis of the obtained data, significant relationships between the variables were determined, e.g. the type of organisational culture and the type of organisation in which the study had been conducted.

Tab. 1: Opinions of organisational leaders in public institutions on the current (O-Hierarchy) organisational culture. Source: own study based on research

	ANOVA of Kruskal-Wallis ranks; O-HIERARCHY Independent variable (grouping): Organisation Kruskal-Wallis test: H (2, N = 335) = 41,09490 p = ,0000			
Dependent: O-HIERARCHY	Code	N significant	Sum of Ranks	Average Rank
1	1	92	19719,00	214,3370
2	2	139	18364,00	132,1151
3	3	104	18197,00	174,9712

Tab. 2: Opinions of organisational leaders in public institutions on the desired future and ideal (P-Hierarchy) organisational culture. Source: own study based on research

	ANOVA of Kruskal-Wallis ranks; P-HIERARCHY Independent variable (grouping): Organisation Kruskal-Wallis test: H (2, N = 335) = 39,95974 p = , 0000			
Dependent: P-HIERARCHY	Code	N significant	Sum of Ranks	Average Rank
1	1	92	19010,00	206,6304
2	2	139	18225,00	131,1151
3	3	104	19045,00	183,1250

It was observed that organisational leaders in public institutions clearly indicate that they prefer hierarchy culture in both the current organisation (O-Hierarchy – Tab. 1) and in the desired/ideal organisation of the future (P-Hierarchy – Tab. 2). The results confirm that people functioning in public institutions, including the surveyed organisational leaders, value order and regularity at work. By choosing the hierarchy culture as desirable, they confirm that they do not see any other possibility of managing the institution and its organisational units, managing people or applying HR solutions already existing in numerous companies of all sizes in Poland.

Features of adhocracy culture (both current O-adhocracy – Tab. 3, and desired P-adhocracy – Tab. 4) and market culture (current O-market – Tab. 5, desired P-market – Tab. 6), definitely the least consistent with the actual state and ideas of the organisational leaders in the public institutions, are included in the tool. Opinions about adhocracy culture and market culture – both present and desired – interpreted together, show that local government offices in Poland are still not adapting to the changing market requirements and expectations of

Tab. 3: Opinions of organisational leaders in public institutions on the current (O-Adhocracy) organisational culture. Source: own study based on research

Dependent: O-ADHOCRACY	ANOVA of Kruskal-Wallis ranks; O-ADHOCRACY Independent variable (grouping): Organisation Kruskal-Wallis test: H (2, N = 335) = 15,05710 p = , 0005			
	Code	N significant	Sum of ranks	Average Rank
1	1	92	12454,00	135,3696
2	2	139	25653,00	184,5540
3	3	104	18173,00	174,7404

Tab. 4: Opinions of organisational leaders in public institutions about the desired future and ideal (P-Adhocracy) organisational culture. Source: own study based on research

Dependent: P-ADHOCRACY	ANOVA of Kruskal-Wallis ranks; P-ADHOCRACY Independent variable (grouping): Organisation Kruskal-Wallis test: H (2, N= 335) = 21,22366 p =, 0000			
	Code	N significant	Sum of ranks	Average Rank
1	1	92	11947,00	129,8587
2	2	139	26276,00	189,0360
3	3	104	18057,00	173,6250

Tab. 5: Opinions of organisational leaders in public institutions on the current (O-Market) organisational culture. Source: own study based on research

Dependent: O-MARKET	ANOVA of Kruskal-Wallis ranks; O-MARKET) Independent variable (grouping): Organisation Kruskal-Wallis test: H (2, N = 335) = 65,10595 p = , 0000			
	Code	N significant	Sum of ranks	Average Rank
1	1	92	12041,00	130,8804
2	2	139	30371,00	218,4964
3	3	104	13868,00	133,3462

Tab. 6: Opinions of organisational leaders in public institutions on the desired future and ideal (P-Market) organisational culture. Source: own study based on research

	ANOVA of Kruskal-Wallis ranks; P-MARKET) Independent variable (grouping): Organisation Kruskal-Wallis test: H (2, N = 335) = 73,37899 p = ,0000			
Dependent: P-MARKET	Code	N significant	Sum of ranks	Average Rank
1	1	92	11545,00	125,4891
2	2	139	30737,00	221,1295
3	3	104	13998,00	134,5962

customers. The local government unit is not a place where modern solutions in the field of HR management would be applied, which require a high level of employee involvement, delegation of privileges, greater autonomy and responsibility. Studies of local government office workers in Poland (previously indicated in this chapter), in terms of their attitudes towards work (implemented in 2006–2016), confirm that most of them expect a style of work, remuneration (basic wage) and other elements of the personnel function to the extent they are currently being offered and enforced (Haromszeki, 2016). It seems particularly important in this context that the organisational leaders (not only formal managers and employees) also feel the most comfortable in this type of relationship.

In the "clan culture" category, in comparison with the leaders operating in the private and non-government sector, organisational leaders in public institutions obtained an average result (current O-Clan – Tab. 7, desirable P-Clan – Tab. 8). The most common answers are not surprising: the highest results occurred in non-governmental organisations created around shared values and being the quintessence of cooperation and team spirit. However, in local government units, the result is definitively higher than in companies. This confirms the nature of work in a public institution coinciding with the expectations of employees, relying on the willingness to cooperate in a good atmosphere in conditions of stability and a high predictability of behaviour.

The results obtained in each type of organisation in the context of the current and desired organisational culture are consistent. This indicates a high homogeneity of the individual groups.

Another aspect of the leadership relationship in public organisations is the question of attitudes towards freedom. The sense of freedom can affect the

Tab. 7: Opinions of organisational leaders in public institutions on the current (O-Clan) organisational culture. Source: own study based on research

	ANOVA of Kruskal-Wallis ranks; O-CLAN Independent variable (grouping): Organisation Kruskal-Wallis test: H (2, N = 335) = 22,89443 p = ,0000			
Dependent: O-CLAN	Code	N significant	Sum of ranks	Average Rank
1	1	92	15977,00	173,6630
2	2	139	19515,00	140,3957
3	3	104	20788,00	199,8846

Tab. 8: Opinions of organisational leaders in public institutions on the desired future and ideal (P-Clan) organisational culture. Source: own study based on research

	ANOVA of Kruskal-Wallis ranks; O-CLAN Independent variable (grouping): Organisation Kruskal-Wallis test: H (2, N = 335) = 16,76412 p = ,0002			
Dependent: P-CLAN	Code	N significant	Sum of ranks	Average Ran
1	1	92	16314,00	177,3261
2	2	139	19913,00	143,2590
3	3	104	20053,00	192,8173

unconventional nature of decisions made and the promotion of proactive and creative behaviours that in some cases lead to creating solutions characteristic of creative destruction.

The sense of organisational leaders' freedom was compared with the assessment of the existing organisational culture and the desired cultural option in the perspective of five years. After analysis of the significance test, it was noticed that in the subscales of O-CLAN, P-CLAN, O-HIERARCHY and P-HIERARCHY, a higher score is reached by leaders who claim that they "mostly feel free" as opposed to those who have a "strong sense of freedom" (Tab. 9).

In the subscales of O-ADHOCRACY and P-ADHOCRACY and O-MARKET and P-MARKET, very rarely chosen by organisational leaders in public institutions, people with a "strong sense of freedom" achieve higher scores than people who say they "mostly feel free" (Tab. 5). These results confirm a specific approach to freedom in local government units, in which subordination to the principles is a determinant of power, belonging and the stabilisation expected by all.

Tab. 9: The sense of freedom of organisational leaders in public institutions and their preferences in the field of organisational culture.
Source: own study based on research

	Mann-Whitney's U test (with continuity correction) Relative to the variable: Freedom The selected results are important from p < ,05000								
Variable	Sum of ranks Group 1	Sum of ranks Group 2	U	Z	p	with correct.	p	N signif. Group 1	N signif. Group 2
O-CKLAN	28386,50	28566,50	12276,50	−2,08845	0,036758	−2,08926	0,036685	179	158
O-ADHOCRACY	32823,50	24129,50	11568,50	2,88170	0,003956	2,88694	0,003890	179	158
O-MARKET	33475,50	23477,50	10916,50	3,61220	0,000304	3,62565	0,000288	179	158
O-HIERARCHY	27330,00	29623,00	11220,00	−3,27216	0,001067	−3,28845	0,001008	179	158
P-CLAN	27804,50	29148,50	11694,50	−2,74052	0,006134	−2,74156	0,006115	179	158
P-ADHOCRACY	34049,50	22903,50	10342,50	4,25532	0,000021	4,26041	0,000020	179	158
P-MARKET	34335,50	22617,50	10056,50	4,57576	0,000005	4,62100	0,000004	179	158
P-HIERARCHY	27185,00	29768,00	11075,00	−3,43462	0,000593	−3,54071	0,000399	179	158

5 Summary

The research conducted in public organisations strongly suggests that the dominant organisational culture is the culture of hierarchy. This culture, as defined earlier in this chapter, is characterised by "a highly formalised workplace with a strict hierarchy in place." The dominance of this type of culture in public institutions is not surprising, as it results from the specifics of the existing way of working in local government units in Poland. It may be surprising, however, that the modernisation of local government offices observed over the last dozen or so years and the implementation of solutions characteristic of the business sector are not applicable to the modification of schematic power or communication structures towards greater use and appreciation of employee potential. In such a system, implementing any ideas from the field of human capital management, including, e.g. using the tool to measure and evaluate human capital[1] in the organisation, does not make sense.

Likewise, there is no doubt that in the local government offices "everything is ruled by procedures." It is an immanent factor of the public sector. Unfortunately, the relationship between the institution and the customer is not fully implemented by Art. 7 of the Constitution of the Republic of Poland – "Public authority bodies operate on the basis and within the limits of the law." (http://www.lexlege.pl/konstytucja-rzeczypospolitej-polskiej/art-7/) In fact, it happens that the actions of officials do not meet the expectations and needs of citizens, although the orientation of people in dealing with various stakeholders would not be a violation of the law. The hierarchy culture is not a factor hampering the achievement of goals in public institutions, because successful leaders selected for the study "are good coordinators and organisers focused on efficiency" – of course, in the sense of efficient functioning of the organisation and consistency with formal rules and regulations. The surveyed leaders, according to previously conducted research with people from their environment (employees of the organisation and members of the local community) (Haromszeki, 2016), create specific leadership relationships, although like other managers (presidents of cities, mayors, heads of departments, managers of teams, office bosses,

1 The tool for measuring and valuating human capital was developed thanks to the cooperation of the Polish Agency for Enterprise Development and the Warsaw School of Economics, as part of the project "Human capital as an element of enterprise value," co-financed by the European Social Fund. The co-author of this study was one of the main experts responsible for testing and implementing the tool, and for promotional and training activities in the project.

etc.), they perform similar tasks in accordance with the legal provisions existing in Poland. The obtained results confirm that organisational leaders, in accordance with the employees' expectations, care about stability, efficiency and work without disruptions. Employee management focuses on employment security, ensuring stability and predictability, which also manifests itself in opinions on the desired organisational culture.

The ideal, desirable type of organisational culture chosen by leaders is certainly a more interesting phenomenon to analyse than a description of the current state. The indication of long-term solutions is an important stage in the process of creating a specific long-term, multi-span leadership relationship in a public organisation. The recognition of the hierarchy as the only possible type of organisational culture employed in public institutions means that any predicted plans to dynamize, streamline or rationalise local government offices in order to modify the existing personnel function seem impossible to implement. Outlining a clear vision of development towards the democratisation of the supervisor-subordinate relationship could positively affect the more conscious and purposeful elimination of competence gaps and the creation of proactive attitudes in public organisations. The implementation of solutions characteristic of the concept of human capital could support the process of building a positive image of the organisation by improving the quality of work. The increase in work efficiency could be the result of the modification of the employee selection and development process, implementation of integrated motivating systems (material and non-material) and solutions in the field of work-life balance (including flexible work forms). The above-mentioned proposals may be used in public organisations if there is an increase in the sense of freedom and the need for employee participation. Such changes, in turn, are likely to occur only when the new way of thinking and acting begins to be the immanent feature of the leaders.

If the future conditions of the leadership relationship are identical with the present ones, this attachment to the hierarchy and a strong reluctance to implement solutions characteristic of adhocracy and market cultures may significantly hinder the functioning of enterprising, creative people, innovators and visionaries in local government units. Such an approach can make any improvements in the local government office operations more difficult to implement, and conducting customer satisfaction surveys will remain only a cunning way of building a positive, though often untrue, image of a given public organisation. Instead of rewarding people who are particularly active as part of a systematic approach to motivating employees, people showing initiative will be discouraged from acting and reduced to average activity in the office. It is difficult to expect public institutions to prefer competition over cooperation, but bypassing market factors may disrupt the process of gaining market positions. Competing for resources, especially funds from the European Union, has already become an important factor in the success of organisational leaders in local government units and, as a result, in the development of local communities led by them.

As the research shows, organisational leaders who prefer the culture of the hierarchy differ significantly in their perception of freedom from respondents active in the adhocracy and market cultures, deliberately giving up on it in order to operate peacefully in such a defined leadership relationship. This stems from the beliefs of leaders that the office is a workplace, which, as a rule, limits the freedom of decision-making, and anyone who decides to work in a public organisation should accept the loss of freedom to a greater extent than it happens in the business sector. This leadership approach may be the main factor hindering the introduction of changes in public organisations.

6 Conclusion

Analysing the research findings on employee expectations towards their superiors and the study of organisational leaders in public institutions, it is not surprising that efficient and effective leadership of people in the culture of hierarchy ensures continuity of the leadership relationship, with the stable approval of supporters. An effective leader in this approach is a professional who fits well into social expectations in terms of predictability and regularity of tasks, stability of employment and maintaining a work atmosphere which is distinctly different from the "rat race" characteristic for corporations. Naturally, the functioning of the leader and employees (subordinates) in such a structure requires restricting the freedom in the scope of making decisions and implementing new solutions. It seems, however, that pragmatic, effective leaders in public organisations, assessing their predispositions as well as the possibilities and approaches of their subordinates, concluded that the relations expected by both parties should still be based on a clear hierarchy. Such an approach reduces organisational chaos and facilitates work, which is to a large extent a schematic reproduction of activities based on the top-down provisions of law. This situation may be altered only as a result of changes taking place on the labour market. The main problems anticipated on the labour market and in various types of organisations in Poland include employee selection and retention as well as the probable decrease in the number of people primarily seeking stability in their job.

In the near future, the above-mentioned problems will probably cause the offices to lose employees, especially those, who, on a relatively stable labour market (also in private organisations), will look for better-paid jobs with greater development opportunities.

In a situation where public institutions lose the main factor affecting their attractiveness on the labour market, e.g. stability of employment in the atmosphere of cooperation, there will probably be an increase of interest in implementing solutions in the field of human capital management in the organisation. This approach may allow for changes in the conditions and employment relationships due to the requirements of the current and anticipated market situation (in particular on the labour market). Among the basic tasks expected to be necessary for the implementation of the so-called Office of the Future, the following should be included: forward thinking (personnel strategy), reduction of formalisation and introduction of a task/ project approach, ongoing research of competency gaps and introduction of new solutions in the field of training (employee development), modifications in motivational systems strengthening the culture of cooperation, but also changing the approach to a more proactive one, resulting in increased efficiency, commitment and creativity.

Literature

Bass B. M., Bass and Stogdill's *Handbook of Leadership: Theory, Research and Managerial Applications*, Free Press, New York 1990.

Cameron K. S., Quinn R. E., *Kultura organizacyjna – diagnoza i zmiana*, Oficyna Ekonomiczna, Kraków 2006.

Chełpa S., *Kierowanie ludźmi i przywództwo*, [in:] T. Listwan T. (red.), Zarządzanie Kadrami(red.), Zarządzanie Kadrami C. H. Beck, Warszawa, 2010.

Den Hartog D. N., Koopman P. P., Thierry H., Wilderom C. P. M., Mączyński J. i Jarmuż S., Dutch and Polish perception of leadership and culture, *European Journal of Work and Organizational Psychology*, 1997, no. 6. 387–413.

Drucker, P. F. *Zawód menedżer*, Wyd. MT Biznes, Konstancin-Jeziorna, 2004.

Fromm E., *Man for Himself*, Rinehart and Comp, New York-Toronto 1947.

Griffin R. W., *Podstawy zarządzania organizacjami*, PWN, Warszawa 1997.

Hall R. J., Workman J. W., Marchioro C. A., Sex, task and behavioural flexibility effects and leadership perceptions, *Organizational Behavior and Human Decision Processes*, Vol. 74, 1998.

Haromszeki Ł., *Przywództwo w czasie kryzysu*, [in:] T. Listwan, (red.), *Zarządzanie w sytuacjach kryzysowych podczas Euro 2012*, Wydawnictwo Uniwersytetu Ekonomicznego we Wrocławiu, Wrocław 2010.

Haromszeki Ł., Expected features and the behavior of talented leaders in the three sectors of the Polish economy in context with other Central-Eastern European countries, *Journal of Intercultural Management* (red. Ł. Sułkowski), 6/4 Grudzień 2014.81–100.

Haromszeki Ł., *Rola przywódców organizacyjnych w kształtowaniu postaw wobec pracy*, [in:] Sukces w zarządzaniu kadrami. Dylematy zarządzania kadrami w organizacjach krajowych i międzynarodowych. Problemy zarządczo-psychologiczne (red. M. Stor, A. Formalczyk), Prace Naukowe Uniwersytetu Ekonomicznego we Wrocławiu, nr. 430, Wrocław 2016a.

Haromszeki Ł., *Oczekiwania wobec przywódców organizacyjnych w opinii studentów zarządzania*, Perspektywy spojrzenia na czynniki sukcesu organizacji XXI wieku, [in:] H. Czubasiewicz, P. Grajewski, J. Waśniewski (red.), Perspektywy spojrzenia na czynniki sukcesu organizacji XXI wieku, Wydział Zarządzania Uniwersytetu Gdańskiego, Sopot 2016b.

Haromszeki Ł., *Preferowane style kierowania w organizacjach trzech sektorów gospodarki*, [in:] K Wojtaszczyk, Zarządzanie różnorodnością w teorii i praktyce, Wydawnictwo SIZ, ..., Łódź 2017.

Hogan R., Curphy G. L., Hogan J., What we know about leadership: Effectiveness and personality, *American Psychologist*, Vol. 49/6, 1994. 493–504.

Hogg M. A., Martin R., Weeden K., Epitropaki O., *Effective Leadership Salient Groups: Revisiting Leader-Member Exchange Theory from the Perspective of the Social Identity Theory of Leadership*, University of Queensland, Queensland 2001.

Kets de Vries M., *Mistyka przywództwa*. Wiodące zachowania w przedsiębiorczości, Wydawnictwo Studio Emka, Warszawa 2008.

Konstytucji RP, art. 7, http://www.lexlege.pl/konstytucja-rzeczypospolitej-polskiej/art-7/).

Kouzes J. M., Posner B. Z., *Przywództwo i jego wyzwania*, Wydawnictwo Uniwersytetu Jagiellońskiego, Kraków 2010.

Koźmiński, A. K. *Zarządzanie w warunkach niepewności*, Warszawa 2004.

Koźmiński A. K., Piotrowski W. (red.), *Zarządzanie. Teoria i Praktyka*, PWN, Warszawa 2006.

Kuc B. R., *Od zarządzania do przywództwa*, Wyd. Menedżerskie PTM, Warszawa 2006.

Kuc B. R., Moczydłowska J. M., *Zachowania organizacyjne*, Difin, Warszawa 2009.

Lord R. S., Foti R. J., DeVader C. L., A test of leadership categorization theory: Internal structure, information processing and leadership perceptions, *Organizational Behavior and Human Performance*, Vol. 34/3, 1984. 343–378.

Mączyński J., Wyspiański D., Differences on organizational practices and preferred leader attributes between Polish managers studies in 2010/2011 and 1996/1997, *Journal of Intercultural Management*, Vol. 3, Number 2, November 2011, s. 7–19.

Prentice W. C. H., *Understanding Leadership*, Harvard Business Review, June 1961, 102-109.

Schein E., *Organization Culture and Leadership. A Dynamic View*, Jossey-Bass, San Francisco 1985.

Sikorski C., *Organizacje bez wodzów. Od przywództwa emocjonalnego do koordynacji demokratycznej*, Wyd. C.H. Beck, Warszawa 2006.

Sims H. P., Manz Ch. C., *Company of Heroes. Unleashing the Power of Self-Leadership*, J. Wiley and Sons, New York 1996.

Yukl G. A., *Leadership in Organizations*, Prentice- Hall, Englewood Cliffs 1989.

Zaccaro S. J., Foti R. J., Kenny D. A., Self-monitoring and trait-based variance in leadership: an investigation of leader flexibility across multiple group situations, *Journal of Applied Psychology*, Vol. 76 (2), 1991. 308–315.

Michał Chmielecki

Leading the Eastern Way: Chinese Philosophy and Innovation

"Business, as well as any other form of organization, must be oriented towards change today - it must be one of their basic activities. They have to induce change, not just respond to it"

Peter Drucker

Abstract: The paper is a discussion with the theory that China has achieved its position on the global market only thanks to adapting the Western style of thinking and doing business. The author gives suggestions why exactly China is such an important partner in a business world and what the role of its philosophical system is. He also depicts the impact of obeying the Confucianism and Daoism rules on creativity development and management by employees.

Keywords: Chinese labor market, philosophical system, transformation, creativity, innovativeness

Introduction

Fueled by a period of explosive growth, China has successfully transformed its role in the global economy. Today, China has expanded beyond manufacturing and emerged as an important player in the information age, adding software, hardware, and service solutions to its well-honed manufacturing capabilities. It is hard to pick a country that has successfully undergone such a radical transformation in such a short period of time. For the last 30 years, China has been a wonder of the worldwide economy. Its annual growth rate has reached an average of 10 %. In 2010, China overtook Japan as the second-largest economy in the world. In the recent 2008–2009 international financial crisis and recession, China performed better than the West. Chinese entrepreneurs, inventors, and scientists are now at the forefront of groundbreaking companies and research institutes. Chinese government ministries are now creating programs to gain technological advantages in clean energy, supercomputers, medicine, and other fields in addition to national defense (Chmielecki, 2012b).

One of the main factors contributing to the country's development is its businesses competitiveness, regarding both domestic and international markets. Innovativeness is one of the elementary factors influencing the company's competitive potential. Innovativeness denotes a tendency and an ability to create and increase value and novelty of produced goods, new or altered technological processes, or organizational and technical modes of management and motivation.

High market unpredictability, as well as its enormous complexity, forces organizations to undertake certain innovative actions, which determine the necessity to create, develop, utilize, and protect their intellectual capital – i.e., non-material and knowledge-related assets. Every company needs to constantly evolve when operating in the markets, in which the external environmental conditions are determined mainly by the processes of globalization and competitiveness. When you additionally consider a shortening product life cycle, you might reach the conclusion that companies ought to more explicitly focus on investments regarding new technologies, advancement of business models, and development of intellectual capital. In our present environment of instant access to information, rapid change, innovation, and communication can be critical to a company's continued existence (Chmielecki, 2016).

Business organizations that are interested in launching into the future must see innovation as a key solution, especially in today's ever-changing business world. Though lots of cultural qualities are essential to construct a suitable environment for innovation, the most important by far is communication. By taking a real interest in the growth of all levels of the business and promoting open communication, employees will have the inspiration and drive to develop groundbreaking and fresh ideas.

As the time for capitalizing on innovations reduces and the speed of innovation becomes even faster, becoming a competitively unpredictable organization is key to running a successful business in the decades ahead. The core of outmaneuvering the competition in ways that they can never see coming is, evidently, robust innovation traditions that set the correct conditions and framework for breakthrough, fast-paced innovation to flourish.

Despite a lot of tremendous economic growth, a lot of people still criticize China for allowing its traditional culture to stop its innovation. However, Chinese culture is now adapting in response to basic technological and economic changes, and its philosophy is not the same as its culture. This chapter was written to show how an irregular combination of philosophical systems from China can bring about creative opportunities in the 21st-century business world (Chmielecki, 2012b).

China's shift from a copycat country to a tech and innovation powerhouse is no longer an aspiration – it's a fact. Both major forces – i.e. consumer appetite and government support – led to the creation of new technologies, industries and the domestic dominance of Chinese firms in existing areas of technology.

1 Key factors contributing to innovativeness

Innovativeness is determined by a broad spectrum of factors that can be analyzed as barriers and stimulants. Innovation can be considered a technical as well as social phenomenon. It is an internal process, at the same time technical and social, equally cultural and organizational – it is a result of real processes and not only apparent behaviors. According to A. Pomykalski, innovation is a process that involves every activity related to the creation of an idea, development of an invention, and introduction of an updated product or service (Pomykalski, 2001).

Innovation can be analyzed from many different methodological standpoints. Psychology treats this concept mainly in terms of individual ingenuity, talent, and their causes. Psychology identifies innovativeness as creative output which encapsulates the creativity, ingenuity, and novelty – i.e., one's abilities to think divergently and take risk. Sociology sees innovativeness as a function of the social system or as a result of social reality-defining processes (Chmielecki, 2013).

The level of innovativeness depends on both exogenous and endogenous factors. Exogenous factors include, for instance, technological, sociocultural, or macroeconomical preconditions. Endogenous factors are understood mainly in terms of economic, intellectual, or psychological determinants.

Although the biggest barriers for development of innovativeness are supposedly capital barriers, namely high costs of initializing innovative activity and limited access to research and development funding, cultural factors also play a vital role in the process.

Innovation is the application of a better solution to meet new requirements, unarticulated needs, or existing market needs. The elements of innovative companies are as follows:

- A winning business strategy
- Great talent
- A valued and empowered workforce
- The free flow of ideas
- Open communication
- Customer insight
- Quality capabilities

Innovation needs its own sole set of skills and company structures. There is no remarkable method in creating a culture of innovation. Establishing one and making it stick depends on understanding the climate. How is the firm going to react throughout periods of experimentation? Which behaviors, structures, goals, and people should be in place to unlock innovation? And which, if positioned improperly, would create discord?

Innovation is not just a pet project. From R&D to human assets, consumer service to financial procedures, success depends on a continuous assessment of creativity – it is everybody's job, all the time.

Innovation is not a rare quality characteristic in a lucky few – it is a way of behaving and thinking that comes to us naturally. An organization's duty is to foster the correct climate to let loose its employees' instinctive ground-breaking tendencies. Innovation needs strong leadership with a solid vision through business. The inner principles of a business together with the outer culture through which it operates will sway a business's capacity to transform.

Innovation flourishes in a culture that is not afraid of taking risks, thus promoting the value of experimenting, and is adaptable and therefore rewards enterprise. Innovation generally wants to be led from the top administration of the business.

The apportionment of resources for innovation includes personnel and finance, and it is reliant on management thus understanding the benefits of new concepts. Regrettably, business overheads on innovation are often characterized as outflow rather than regarded as investment, and progresses to operational procedures are not seen as innovation at all. Income needs to be allotted to innovation, even if it just allows the staff time to cultivate fresh ideas.

A free flow of data and concepts up, down, and across the business inspire the growth of new ways of carrying out tasks and can lead to the growth of new products. Practices which enable employees to suggest ideas and developments, circulate these concepts and be content with their entrepreneurial behavior can be effected.

Modern times are so dynamic that currently change is the most unchanging phenomenon. Every day introduces us to new products, new businesses, and changes to our economic situation. Changes in technology make it necessary to deploy new solutions and continually develop employees through training in order to keep up with the competition. Changes occur everywhere: in the environment, in the economy, in politics, in culture, and in society. The implementation of new solutions is commonplace in both microcompanies and large corporations. Those who benefit from this dynamic are the people who can foresee changes in both the external and internal surroundings of the company.

They aptly analyze this information and adequately implement carefully measured changes.

2 Culture and philosophy are different

The popular Western view is that almost all of China's achievement in recent times is due to its conversion to Western ways of thought and business philosophy. There are even some Chinese people, mostly those living in America, who doubt that lessons learned in their ancient philosophical schools can be applicable in the business world. Is it possible that the philosophical part of this culture can play a great part in providing chances of creativity in today's business world?

A piece of the problem lies in the fact that the lessons from some philosophical founders from over 2000 years ago have become distorted and covered up by bureaucratic practices and cultural traditions of patriarchal families from China. The ruling families in China usually blend Confucian values of reciprocity and humanity with the Legalist school principle of total power.

There is a practical way of examining Chinese philosophy from a mission-focused perspective of business. There are obviously major principles that are flexible and reasonable in today's economic world, as well as the teachings that are useful from various Chinese schools, mostly Daoism and Confucianism, which can be applied to business from a technological and a managerial point of view.

Now, one can talk about Chinese philosophy from a more high-tech and competitive point of view without bringing in unchanging traditions from an era that started before the industrial age. One must recognize that today's China has conditions that are greatly different from the China of yesterday. The current social hierarchies that exist in China of today do so in capitalist state-owned business ventures and not within stagnant, conventional rural families. This is proof that you can now restate Chinese philosophy from a more high-tech, competitive economic perspective. It is visible that no one can state that the values present in Chinese philosophy can be totally cut away from aged methods in Chinese culture. How beneficial this philosophy could be for a business should be examined, given that the technological and economic foundations of Chinese culture have changed greatly over the last generation. There is much greater fluidity of movement in present-day China.

3 The major principles of Chinese philosophy for today's business

There are two main schools of philosophical thought that originated from China in the middle of the first millennium BC. They are Daoism (or Taoism) and

Confucianism. Buddhism is a third main school of thought that was exported to China from Southern Asia in the first few hundred years of the first millennium CE. Later, there was a confluence between the principles of these three schools of thought.

Daoism and Confucianism proffer various causal worldviews and social values which, when blended, can whip up various avenues of creativity within business settings. Looking at this from a business perspective, the blending of these two schools creates a philosophical system that is more advantageous than taking the principles of each school as a separate entity. This happens as a result of the fact that a business concern operates at the same time in various economical, technological, and social environments.

4 Confucian dissimilarity and concord

Now that Confucianism is enjoying a massive renaissance in China and various Confucius Institutes throughout the world, which major values does it offer the business community? In the West, Confucianism is usually illustrated as a kind of tradition-obsessed, rigid, inferior subordinate system, especially in the Chinese family. There is much more to Confucian values than a basic principle of ranking. Also, in the China of today, business organizations – not families – rule the social ranking system. The rigid, rural family is no longer the basic unit of production in the present-day economy of China. Millions of rural Chinese people have moved to urban areas in search of work for large export-based manufacturing organizations. Therefore, it is worth asking if Chinese philosophy can provide a means for innovation in newly educated, high-tech, urbanized, change-focused business organizations. The Confucianist system admonishes a reasonable and humanitarian approach to relationships among all people and in various business settings. Confucianism does not apply to ruling entities and family alone. It shares the thought that human nature is basically good. It also places a high thought value on harmony, reciprocity, and honesty among ranks, and it encourages good work ethics. Rank between organizations should be determined by capability and merit – not by wealth, friendship, or ancestral background.

The Confucian system has a principle of respect for superiors, but it is more intricate than this. There is a Confucian saying stating that irrespective of our differences, we should work together for the good of the organization. It advocates that everyone in business firms should work in conjunction with each other while understanding different points of views and statuses. Respect is reciprocal. The perfect Confucian way of doing business advocates a great level of unity between employees at various levels, instead of just obeying a simple one-directional chain of command.

This reciprocal approach to hierarchy is different in various places, at least in theory, from the traditional top-down Weberian form of office bureaucracy common in the West. A clear hierarchy still exists, but the perfect Confucian business setting has a high level of unity and cooperation between employees at various rungs on the corporate ladder. This will boost productivity greatly and create greater sharing of technology, information, research, and other resources, therefore providing more means for innovation. This will be useful for meeting today's economic climate of rapid change and enhanced global competition (Chmielecki, 2007).

Apart from increasing the value of reciprocity in the business hierarchy, in the *Analects*, Confucius advocates everyone to seek truth and knowledge. Everyone should question others eagerly to avoid premature conclusions and erratic assumptions. Everyone should think for themselves. Employees of various status should accept critique willingly. In the old dynasties of imperial China, the proper Confucian advisers were always watchful and did not refrain from giving advice to the emperor. According to John Keay (2009), who wrote *China: A History*, obedience to superiors does not stop any constructive form of protest. A model Confucian ruler should be kind and morally upright. He must care for the welfare of his subjects. In the business world of today, conjunct criticism can promote the creation of substitute ideas in management and research teams. These teams will then become more important to the company than ever before.

5 Effortless mastery of Daoism

Confucianism is not the only organic philosophical school of thought in China that has the potential to be used in management and business. Daoism, also known as Taoism, is another Chinese philosophical school of thought. Confucianism is majorly applied to the relationship between people, while Daoism centers around the relationship of an individual with his natural and physical world. In modern business, this relationship covers the entire economical and technological environment. These include suppliers, banks, customers, competing firms, government agencies, and sources of service and product technology (Chmielecki, 2012b).

Fernand Braudel (1995), in *A History of Civilizations*, presented the view of Joseph Needham (1974) – prominent historian of Chinese science – who stated that China's organic view of the world is the same as that which science is turning to currently. This is far different to the mechanistic view of Newton, which was commonplace until the end of the 19th century. Joseph Needham shared the point of view that Daoism was a major source of inspiration for Chinese science in the era before the modern one. Jacques Gernet, a popular historian, wrote that China does not like the idea of not having an opposition or the idea of an absolute idea. China likes a distinction between matter and mind. China prefers the idea of circulation, complementarity, a model, inflow of action at a distance, and the idea of an organic totality (Gernet, 1996).

The major Daoist values are harmony, dynamic balance, and holism. One should work and live in peace with every aspect of the environment. To learn Daoism means to understand the Dao: the central life force or way of nature. Nature arrives at an organic balance between different forces. How will one blend with nature? That kind of learning is a form of ecological study. It is a gentle impassive process. One must seek to understand the environment and all the interrelationships so well, that to outsiders his or her doing so will appear effortless. Followers of Daoism describe this process as wuwei or "doing by not doing." Students of Daoism hope to arrive at a point where they are either superiorly aware or where they trust their instinct to understand their environment fully. Speaking modernly, this point includes an awareness of how the environment changes. This is a natural part of technology and economy as visible in forces of supply and demand in a business organization.

6 Chinese creativity and innovation

Confucianism promotes unity among various people in different levels in the corporate ladder. Although this is usually not practiced in the East, it is not a tradition of the West. In the corporate hierarchies of the West, there is usually a tension among individuals and a feeling of conflict between those in lower and upper positions in an organization. Confucianism can develop a mesh of contacts that create a social capital within an organization. This can become a valuable resource for solving future problems and creativity in various aspects of the operation of a company.

Thus employees in various parts of a country should see that they are similar, and they should cooperate with one another, because they all work together to accomplish the missions and market objectives of a company.

Confucianism, as applied to business, is organic, pure, and nonlinear. Lower and upper positions should complement each other rather than oppose each other. This is a major value of Chinese thought. It is important that you have more similarities than differences. It can be thought of in terms of yin and yang. These are different values that complement each other to make one whole part.

Employees in various segments of a company should see themselves as similar to each other, and thus they should cooperate with one another. They should realize that they share an attachment to the market objectives and mission of a company. If they focus on these goals, they can contribute in various ways towards innovation in a company.

Opposing points of view in business should not be rejected outrightly as is often done in the West. Opposition is a concept whose outlook depends on various perspectives. A Confucian businessman looks for complementary factors and similarities among various opposing points of view. He tries to merge them together to create an innovative blend of various ideas. This approach will significantly increase creative opportunities.

This kind of one-directional and serious learning can bring up a lot of new, creative ideas. Stephen Mitchell, the translator of the Daoist classic *Tao Te Ching*, is of the opinion that staying with the receptive aspect allows the creative nature to flow. The amenable and the creative are sides of the same process that complement each other (Asor, 2010).

Business receptivity should not be left to chance all the time. It can be boosted through focus groups, surveys, and global and domestic research teams that cut across the usual lines of authority, seminars, and brainstorming sessions.

There is a need to have a renewed focus on the company mission. It is needed to become a life force or dao for an innovative business. A mission concept serves as a linkage between various functions, technologies, company units, ideas for change and products. The differences between these complement each other to make a whole organ. This is because of their connection to the mission concept that may evolve over time. There is also a need to adopt social objectives as the company will evolve to blend into its competitive environment.

There is also the need to provide a new economic interpretation for expanding Daoist thought. An organization should always select a perspective that adopts all these external economic factors. Normally, a company's production function should bring in private costs along with social costs. An all-encompassing evaluation of such costs could lead to new breakthroughs in technology. Such examples include new developments in sustainable or green technology – e.g., wind power, carbon capture, and solar power. There has already been monumental progress in green technology by China.

Multinational corporations (MNCs) in China demand a specific type of talented employee. The profile looks as follows: a young, upwardly mobile Chinese professional with advanced technical skills and a solid understanding of international management techniques. They are also expected to possess strong foreign language skills, initiatives, and a strategic mindset. However, MNCs have extreme difficulties in finding these people. The supply of this type of employee is small in the market, since China just has a short history of a market-oriented economy to foster them. Secondly, the market competition for such talent is fierce (Chmielecki, 2012a).

The Chinese universities and colleges have traditionally focused too much on students' "academic skills which motivated students mostly to strive for high scores in exams. However, such education failed to cultivate students' creativity, willingness to risk-taking, leadership, teamwork and other 'soft' qualities and skills that most MNCs would require in the real business world. As a result, although the number of graduate students rises consecutively every year, MNCs have not seen a corresponding increasing pool of qualified talent" (Chmielecki, 2012a).

7 The great Chinese paradox

Opposition could become opportunity because one must look at how various viewpoints complement each other in order to achieve a complex blend of ideas.

The statement above shows a major Chinese paradox. Sometimes, bodies dismiss Chinese philosophy as an undynamic body of thought that strengthens old traditions between institutions, people, and their surroundings. But if one looks beyond the bias that is prevalent and examines individual ways of work behavior in this philosophy, they should be considered separate from old constraints in economic environments. From this, a new point of view will arise. An individual should be ready to work hand in hand with other employees and must also be willing to dish out and receive constructive criticism. Opposition then becomes an opportunity as one begins to examine the similarities and ways by which different points of view augment each other to form a sophisticated blend of ideas. Complexity itself must be accepted as part of the organization's organic view worldwide. An individual must do his/her best to learn the technological process that is involved in the production of a company's products. This must also influence a change in direction in supplier resources, demand from consumers, and competition in business. That kind of learning must take action by foreseeing events, and must be active in many ways. This is the modern result of the Daoist effortless and efficient mastery of nature.

The Asian principles of being congruous while being different, mutual criticism, and total environmental awareness always create a powerful work ethic. This leads to the development of social capital and brings up opportunities for creativity. Today, innovation in organizations is an advanced mix of large teams of engineers, marketing specialists, scientists, and IT specialists. It does not matter if team members are geographically and ethnically widespread. Chinese philosophies provide a means of maximizing the efficiency of personnel and technological resources of an organization. This strategy can now be achieved with IT resources like cloud computing, high-speed internet, simulation, and other resources that reduce previous barriers of information processing and time. The Chinese philosophical system is exacting and intensive, but it provides a lot of creativity for organizations and it is practical for business. There is a balance between these new changes that complement each other. The economic and technological modern business world is less stable and more dynamic and complex. But IT resources and other business resources needed to respond to and dominate this world are now faster, more powerful, and more efficient. The whole method of managing businesses has now changed, and it operates at a higher level of awareness and intensity. The new openings for creativity are now a part of this new intensity.

The recent call for a new dimension in creativity states that business firms will always be confronted by strategic challenges previously unheard of in business history. It is visible that there must be a time-sensitive, holistic, IT-responsive understanding of the consumer, and an economic and technological company environment which is connected to this new challenge. The Chinese philosophical system offers vast guidelines suitable for these situations. It places immense importance on a long-term business value system over short-term gain. The fact that China's economy has been growing very fast is also helpful. But in order to keep up with the high growth in the future, there is a need to search for and master new products, markets, and new ways of saving costs. The "Eastern way" must be an integral part of this process, and not only for China.

8 Summary

The growth of China as one of the world's most powerful nations presents very unique opportunities for MNCs. The role of culture in management has gained in importance (Sułkowski, 2002). Companies that understand cultural nuances, hire the appropriate professionals, are flexible, and can create a sort of a cultural fusion without changing the core values will be successful. The specificity of the Chinese labor market poses key challenges for the success of the MNCs' business operations in China, the main challenges being the shortage of top talent with international experience, the current labor and legal restrictions for recruitment, and retention policy implementation. MNCs have to face those challenges to attract, recruit, and retain their talent, and adapt the related policies to the local institutional environment (Chmielecki, 2012a).

Bibliography

Asor, W. B. (2010). *Entrepreneurship in the Philippines Setting*. New Hampshire: Rex Book Store.

Braudel, F. (1995). *A History of Civilizations* (p. 178). New York: Penguin Books.

Chmielecki, M. (2007). Chiński styl komunikacji interpersonalnej i jego wpływ na negocjacje. *Przedsiębiorczość i Zarządzanie*, *8*(1) s. 294.

Chmielecki, M. (2012a). HR Challenges in China. *Journal of Intercultural Management*, *4*(3), 49–55.

Chmielecki, M. (2012b). Wpływ konfucjanizmu na praktykę zarządzania w Chinach, Przedsiębiorczość i Zarządzanie, 13(13), 7–24.

Chmielecki, M. (2013). Culture as a Barrier of Knowledge Sharing. *Journal of Intercultural Management*, *5*(2), 101–111.

Chmielecki, M. (2017). Knowledge Sharing in MNCs. *Intercultural Interactions in the Multicultural Workplace: Traditional and Positive Organizational Scholarship*, 267–282

Gernet, J. (1996). *A History of Chinese Civilization*. Cambridge: Cambridge University Press.

Needham, J. (1974). *Science and Civilisation in China: Historical Survey, from Cinnabar Elixirs to Synthetic Insulin. Vol. 5, Chemistry and chemical technology; Pt. 3, Spagyrical discovery and invention* (Vol. 3). Cambridge: Cambridge University Press.

Pomykalski, A. (2001). Zarządzanie innowacjami. Warszawa-Łódź: PWN, s. 17.

Sułkowski, Ł. (2002). *Kulturowa zmienność organizacji*. Warszawa: Polskie Wydawnictwo Ekonomiczne.

Sułkowski, Ł., & Chmielecki, M. (2017). Positive Cross-Cultural Scholarship Research.In: *Intercultural Interactions in the Multicultural Workplace: Traditional and Positive Organizational Scholarship*, (Eds.) Rozkwitalska, M., Sułkowski, Ł., Magala, S., Springer, Heilderberg, 19–35.

Sylwia Przytuła

Expatriate Leaders*

Abstract: The diversity of international employees means that organizations face many challenges related to their acquisition, development, motivation and retention. Therefore, the key role is played by expatriate leaders whose multidimensional competences will allow to manage effectively the multicultural teams. The purpose of this chapter is to characterize expatriate leader in relation to normative and competency based- approach.

Keywords: Global leader, leadership theories, expatriate, competency-based approach, cross-cultural leadership

Introduction

Global leadership is emerging as a critical issue in international management because new environmental factors (i.e., globalization, demographic imbalances, military conflicts, technological and competitive pressure) have created a context not previously seen (Clapp-Smith, R., Lester, 2014; International Organization for Migration (IOM), 2016). The scale of international mobility and the intensity of displacement has never been as large as it is today (The United Nations, 2015). In a Cartus survey, half of the companies expect to see mobility volume increase overall for the upcoming 2-year period, and 63 % said global mobility was critically important to strategic global expansion of MNCs (Brookfield, 2016).

Internationalization of enterprises and their expansion into foreign markets cause that mobility also increases among employees who undertake a diversified form and duration of foreign missions. These employees are called "expatriates" (Brewster, 1991; McNulty, Brewster, 2017; Selmer, 1995), but also "global business leaders" (Caligiuri, 2013), "highly mobile managers" (Forster, 2000), "global careerists" (Suutari et.al., 2012), or "glopatriates" (McPhail, 2012).

Companies are focusing on creating a pipeline of future leaders with global management experience (Brookfield, 2016), and the expectations towards the job of a global leader are extensive (Ghemawat, 2012). Overall, 63 % agree or strongly agree that there is an urgent need to develop globally competent leaders (*UNC Leadership Survey 2015*). Some authors also define a "global citizen" as one who honors his/her

* This chapter is part of the "INTEREKON research and development excellence program", financed under the MNISW program under the name "Regional Initiative of Excellence" in the years 2019–2022, project number 15 / RID / 2018/19

own unique origins while developing appreciation of and integration into a larger global citizenship (Rogers, Blonski, 2010). According to 80 % of respondents, global mobility policy facilitates global business initiatives, and nearly half (46 %) of the respondents indicate that such an approach is focused on ensuring globally mobile employees receive optimal levels of service support (Brookfield 2016, p. 16).

As managers around the globe increasingly face the challenges of leading employees from different cultural backgrounds with divergent expectations about hierarchy, power, and interpersonal relations, it becomes important for them to understand how these differences can influence effective leadership (Steers et al., 2012).

The purpose of this chapter is to characterize the expatriate leader in relation to normative and competency-based approaches. The chapter is of a descriptive character and reviews literature on "global leadership" and "expatriate management" to identify key, specific competencies for the "expatriate leader" in response to a growing demand for such international workers.

1 Cross-cultural context of global leadership

Multiculturalism, which is a "demographic feature" of corporate employees (Arasaratnam, 2013), and a unique trait of these globally active actors (Rozkwitalska, Sułkowski, 2016, p. 21), becomes a key challenge for managers (Lauring, Selmer, 2012; Lauring, Selmer, 2011; Przytuła et al., 2014). S. Vertovec (2006) coined the concept of *super diversity*, emphasizing the complexity of contemporary multicultural societies with multiple identities, socially, economically, and legally distinct, whose representatives differ in attitude, acculturation, and length of residence in the host country.

Differences in leadership behavior across cultures have been noticed by a large body of research (Bass, 1990; Selmer, 1996; Smith et al., 1989). The role of culture and how it affects desired and effective leadership have been explored in the Global Leadership and Organizational Behavior Effectiveness (GLOBE) research project, which sought to identify universal leadership attributes. GLOBE found only a small number of universal leadership attributes (e.g., trustworthy, decisive, informed). The majority of leader attributes were culturally contingent and their desirability was significantly related to culture (Dorfman et al., 2012). Such a practice was also proved by Z. Aycan (2008, p. 238): "the most effective leadership style is always that which best fits the cultural context". Several other studies (Engelen et al., 2014; Takahashi et al., 2012) also support the hypothesis that culture affects those perceived to be a leader and what leadership styles look like (Hanges et al., 2016; Mączyński, Sułkowski, 2017).

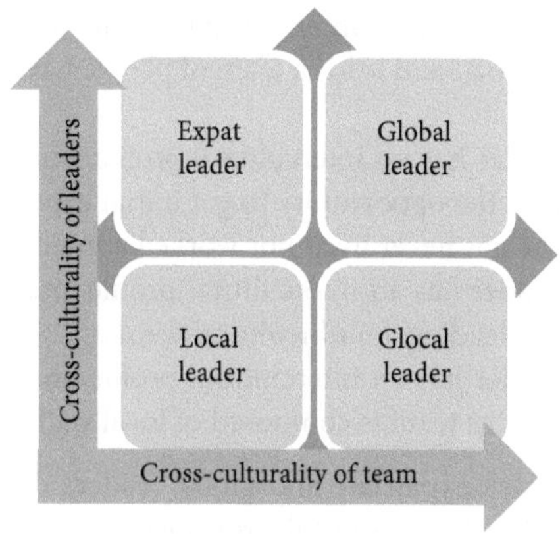

Fig. 1: Global leaders in cultural context. Source: Dziatzko et al. (2016).

How managers from other cultures are perceived has become more important, because more employees than ever before are working for foreign companies and for foreign managers. Although this increasing globalization is certainly not new to the theory, research and practice of leadership and the understanding and dimensions of effective global leadership continued to be a challenge (Youssef, Luthans, 2012). Hence, perceptions about differences in leadership behavior between cultures and their competencies which determine the successful mission abroad are increasingly relevant to international firms. Such perceptions could also influence preferences towards expatriate managers, particularly because a wealth of research findings shows that expatriate managers in foreign assignments typically apply the same leadership approaches as they used in their home country, and do not adjust or adapt to the local norms and practices (Black, Porter, 1991; Lawson, Swain, 1985; Stening, Hammer, 1992). Thus, managers from a different culture could be viewed as less preferable simply because they are perceived as different from local managers, although in J. Selemer's study it was found that the leadership style of the US expatriates was preferred over local bosses' in Hong Kong (Selmer, 1996).

Beechler and Baltzley (2008) differentiate between global and domestic leaders, contending that a global leader chooses from a broader behavioral repertoire than a domestic leader. Based on the model of Dziatzko et al. (2016) four profiles of leaders can be distinguished, depending on two dimensions: their cross-cultural background and the cross-culturality of the team (see Fig. 1):

Local Leader: this leader has no intercultural profile, meaning he has not yet lived and worked abroad and leads a team of people having the same cultural background as himself.

Glocal leader: this leader has no intercultural profile, but leads a multicultural team. This gives him the opportunity to get initial exposure to a foreign culture even though he has never lived nor worked abroad.

Global leader: this leader has an intercultural profile, meaning he is currently working abroad and leading a multicultural team.

Expat Leader: this leader has an intercultural profile, meaning he is currently working abroad, but his team is composed of local staff.

According to the model, expatriate and global leaders do not differ in terms of their cross-culturality (e.g., cultural provenience, international experience, nationality), but the expat manages a culturally homogeneous team, and the global leader is dealing with linguistic, cultural, ethnic, and religious diversity of their employees. Therefore, external factors such as work environment, the team of employees, not internal ones (like personality traits or skills), are factors that differentiate these leaders. However, in management practice, expats also manage a multicultural team and are more effective in this regard, due to their own professional or personal experiences of cultural diversity.

On one hand, research has highlighted a set of specific qualities and intercultural skills that make leaders effective, but on the other hand, leaders work with a diverse group of employees that have different expectations for leadership. These expectations make him more culturally aware, and thus some skills must be developed to match the expectations of the team members.

Ł. Haromszeki (Haromszeki, 2014) pointed out that if people observe behavior consistent with their expectations, they start calling the person behaving that way a leader. Behavior consistent with expectations causes the organizational leader to gain credibility.

Different cultures place different values on different leadership behaviors and values; research has highlighted the importance of cultural sensitivity of leaders (Agrawal, Rook, 2014; *UNC Leadership Survey 2015*). Moreover, a traditional approach to cross-cultural management suggests that to be effective, the leader has to change his/her management style to adapt to new circumstances and to match each member's cultural expectations. Rodsutti and Swierczek (2002) have observed that there is a so-called multicultural leadership style, where the manager who directs the team respects cultural differences, and increases the satisfaction of the staff. But instead of expecting a leader to become a "chameleon", the current research (Clapp-Smith, Lester, 2014; Mendenhall, Bird, 2013; Osland et al., 2012) presents some demanding, core competencies required from all such leaders (Hanges et al., 2016). In this discussion, the author proposes simply a competency approach to global leaders.

2 Existing definitions of "global leaders" and "expatriates"

As globalization leads to a great diversity in the workplace, it can be seen as a cause and effect simultaneously (Scheffer, Werner, 2012). Leaders can be seen as a product of globalization and as a driver, accompanying a change in mindset of the business world (Osland et al., 2017). M.E. Mendenhall and A. Bird pointed to discretion in such word combinations: "global" and "leadership". Some people think "global" is a descriptive term for the nature of work a manager is assigned to accomplish; others think it involves having to interact with clients from other countries; still others see it as a business environment in which they work – that is to say the business world is international in nature (Mendenhall, Bird, 2013).

Tab. 1 provides a sample of definitions of **global leaders** that have been applied by scholars in the field:

Putting all the above definitions into Wordle, some keywords appeared, as shown in Fig. 2.

The lack of specificity is reflected in the use of ambiguous terms to define global leader; however, many other studies do not explicitly state a construct definition of "global leader" or even use this term for defining "expatriate".

The first known use of the word "expatriate" was in 1812 in the Merriam-Webster Dictionary. According to N. Green (2009), from the adoption of the "Expatriation Act" in the United States in 1868, the word "expatriate" was "a disturbing noun denoting a suspicious citizen", and in 1920, the issue of expatriation was expanded from the category of "citizenship" to the category of "a citizen travelling or staying abroad". In contrast to the "outcast" and "lost citizenship" used in the past, the modern status of that term is privileged (Przytuła, 2013a).

The word "expatriate" comes from the Latin expatriātus where "ex" means "out of" and "patriā" means "fatherland". Thus, the origin of the word "expatriate (expat)" means a person leaving their fatherland to live outside it (Oxford Dictionary of English, 2015) or who has been sent or exiled abroad (Collins Dictionaries, 2011). There is also an expatriate definition *sensu largo*, saying that it is a person that has left their homeland, lives and/or works in a country other than their country of origin (Przytuła, 2015).

During nearly a 40-year period, the field of expatriates studies established a core group of early scholars whose names would become synonymous with research about "international executives" (McNulty, Selmer, 2017). Thus an expatriate *sensu stricto* is defined as an employee in an international company,

Tab. 1: Chosen definitions of a "global leader". Source: Mendenhall et al. (2012, p. 495)

Definition of a "global leader"	***Author***
An executive who is in a job with some international scope, whether in an expatriate assignment or in a job dealing with international issues more generally.	(Spreitzer, McCall., Mahoney, 1997)
Global leaders are managers with global integration responsibilities in global organizations.	(Suutari, 2002)
Global executives are those who do global work. With so many kinds of global work, again depending on the mix of business and cultural crossings involved, there is clearly no one type of global executive. Executives, as well as positions, are more or less global depending upon the roles they play, their responsibilities, what they must get done, and the extent to which they cross borders.	(McCall, Hollenbeck, 2002)
Anyone who leads global change efforts in public, private, or nonprofit sectors is a global leader.	(Osland, 2008)
Global leaders, defined as executives who are in jobs with some international scope, must effectively manage through the complex, changing, and often ambiguous global environment.	(Caligiuri, 2006)
Global leaders [are] high-level professionals such as executives, vice presidents, directors, and managers who are in jobs with some global leadership activities such as global integration responsibilities. Global leaders play an important role in developing and sustaining a competitive advantage.	(Caligiuri, Tarique, 2009)
Global leaders are individuals who effect significant positive change in organizations by building communities through the development of trust and the arrangement of organizational structures and processes in a context involving multiple cross-boundary stakeholders, multiple sources of external cross-boundary authority, and multiple cultures under conditions of temporal, geographical, and cultural complexity.	(Mendenhall, M., Oddou, G., Osland, J., Bird, A., Maznevski, 2008)
People in business settings whose job or role is to influence the thoughts and actions of others to achieve some finite set of business goals … usually displayed in large, multicultural contexts.	(Youssef, C., Luthans, 2012).
Global leaders must handle environments that are very different from those that domestic leaders face; they need to confront ongoing change with stakeholders across cross-cultural, geographical, and sociopolitical context.	Roseen, Singer-za mendenhall, s. 496
Global leaders – at whatever level or location – will embrace the challenges of global competition, generate personal and organizational energies to confront those challenges and to transform the organizational energy into world class performance	(Brake, 1997)

Fig. 2: Word cloud for "global leader". Source: www.wordle.net.

usually a top-ranking specialist or manager who is sent from the corporate headquarters to foreign units pursuant to his voluntary decision. An expatriate may come from the home country of the corporate headquarters or be of different nationality than the home country of the corporation (Przytuła, 2015).

Tab. 2 presents chosen definition of an **assigned expatriate** in the literature of the subject.

However, despite more than four decades of research on this population of workers (Dabic et al., 2013; Kraimer et al. 2016), there is still no consensus on theoretical grounds in defining such employees. We are rather dealing with the "jangle fallacy" (Molloy, Ployhart, 2012). There are rather numerous terms of "expatriate" that refer also to the "global leader" or are used interchangeably (Fig. 3).

Putting all the above terms into Wordle, most frequent words appeared, as shown in Fig. 4.

It is worth mentioning that an international career may be achieved through assigned expatriation (AE), in which a plan of foreign assignment for selected employees is generally prepared by an organization, as it was characterized in Tab. 2, but also through **self-initiated expatriation** (SIE) (Al Ariss, Crowley-Henry, 2013; Doherty et al., 2013; Tharenou, Caulfield, 2010). This form of foreign mission means that the initiative to go abroad is undertaken individually by a person that independently (that is without belonging to any organization) seeks out employment in the global market (Przytuła, 2016).

Tab. 2: Chosen definition of an "assigned expatriate". Source: author's own work

Definition of an assigned expatriate	Author
An employee of a business or government organization sent to a country other than their homeland to implement the goals of the organization	(Aycan et al., 2000)
Expatriates are usually the employees working outside the country of their origin (this definition is also reserved for parent country nationals), and sometimes also for (third-country nationals) in foreign branches of their corporation for the period that usually lasts from 2 to 5 years	(Harzing, 2004)
An employee transferred from the home country of the corporation with planned repatriation (position in the company after return) who may come from the home country or the third country	(Ya Ping, 2009)
An employee sent from the country of their origin to another country in which the corporation has its operating units	(Dowling, Festing, 2008)
Expatriates are not usually the citizens of the countries in which they work	(Dessler, 2003)
Like migrants, expatriates have been conceptualized as living somewhere other than their home country – "home" being determined by their passport and citizenship	(Andresen et al., 2014)
Usually relocates abroad for periods of time of between 2 and 5 years, which is in line with them being provided traditional career managements that is controlled and directed by the organization to facilitate a match between organizational and individual needs in pursuit to its continued competitive advantage	(Tharenou, 2013)
An employee temporally transferred abroad by their organization, which arranges and supports the move, to work in a foreign subsidiary for an organizational goal	(Tharenou, 2017)

Another "actor of international mobility" (Kawczyńska-Butrym, 2017) is a **sojourner,** who voluntary and temporarily travels to a foreign country for a nonbusiness purpose such as short-term unpaid missionary and charity work, exile, education, retirement, or simply to see and experience the world (McNulty, Brewster, 2017, p. 57). V. Suutari and C. Brewster also distinguished a **commuter,** who retains permanent residence status in their home country but works, unaccompanied by family members, on a semi-permanent to permanent basis in another country. "Work" includes crossing an international border daily, weekly, or longer periods away due to high-stress expatriation where a family stays in a safer country while the expatriate spends days or weeks in a dangerous one nearby (Suutari, Brewster, 2009).

Fig. 3: Cloud of chosen terms of assigned expatriate in the literature of the subject. Source: McNulty, I., Brewster (2017).

Fig. 4: Word cloud for "expatriate". Source: www.wordle.net.

However, the global leadership requirements will vary significantly for each type of assignee. Someone who regularly travels to a host of different countries grapples more with different leadership demands than someone who always travels to the same country. For example, a self-initiated expatriate, who, after finding an international job on his own, may be more immersed in local responsibilities and untethered to headquarters (Mendenhall et al., 2012).

Moreover, international business is much more personal and relationship-oriented than domestic business. Managers in the global arena require multiple approaches in order to deal with multiple cultures. Those who are skilled only in monocultural management rarely succeed in a multicultural or bicultural environment (Kossek et al., 2017).

3 Contemporary approaches to global leadership

Due to the wide range of definitions related to "global leader" and "expatriate", the common ground for characterizing "expatriate leader" may be the normative approach (Steers et al., 2012) and **competency-based approach** (Kupczyk, Stor, 2017).

The literature of the subject proposed many typologies of leadership theories, beginning from great man theories, trait theories, behaviorist theories, situational leadership, contingency theory, down to transactional and transformational theories (Bolden et al., 2003). There are also some leadership theories that have recently emerged: ethical leadership (Martin et al., 2009), spiritual leadership (Fry, 2003), or authentic leadership (Avolio, Luthans, 2006), contributing to the theory, research, and practice of the subject.

But some researchers suggest another configuration describing the global leadership model, consisting of universal, contingency, and normative approaches (Steers et al., 2012).

3.1 Universal approach

Underlying this approach is the belief that leadership traits and processes are relatively constant across cultures. To this extent that this is correct, the goal of managers is to adopt a leadership model, e.g., charismatic leadership, under the assumption that its applicability is universal regardless of location. Despite decades of research supporting situational approaches to leadership effectiveness, companies still routinely sponsor leadership training programs that stress a few keys to successful leadership and ignore critical variations in local environments (Steers, s. 480).

With respect to global leadership, we have various descriptions of "ideal" or "one best way" of management, which, regardless of the location of the foreign mission, should be effective at every latitude. This approach has been verified in business practice in recent years, proving that the manager's nationality, cultural origin, individual personality traits (Caliuri, 2000), and host country culture determine the success in managing abroad, and the expatriates' adjustment to the host country (Hippler et al., 2017) or their relationships with local staff (Przytula et al., 2014). Such a "culturally-versatile hybrid" has no chance to be performed in a global environment, and a high failure rate of foreign missions

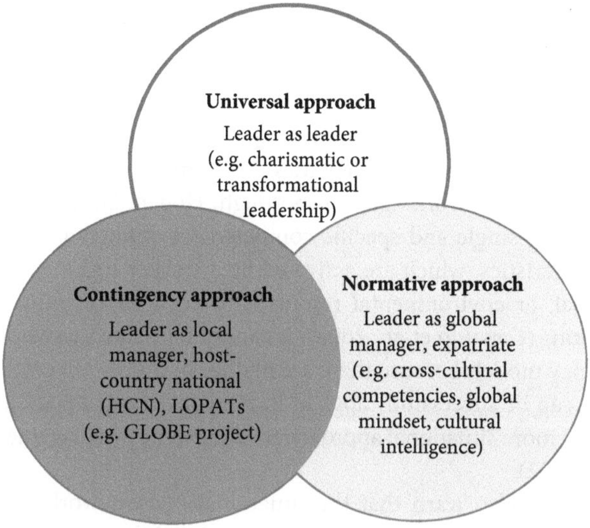

Fig. 5: Contemporary model of global leadership. Source: based on Steers et al. (2012, p. 480).

based on the universal assumption (Brookfield Global Relocation Trends, 2016; Tung, 2016) have further supported the contingency approach.

3.2 Contingency approach

The contingency theory is based on the assumption that successful leaders in New York may fail in Tokyo if they are unable to modify their behavior to suit the unique local environment. Here, the focus is on leaders as local managers, not global ones, and it is assumed that the characteristics for success will vary with the situation (Steers et al., 2012, p. 480). This approach was empirically proved by the GLOBE project (Dorfman et al., 2012; Mączyński, Sułkowski, 2017).

In the literature of expatriation, such an approach may relate to host country nationals (HCN) or localized expatriates (LOPATS), whose importance in successful expatriate management is increasing (*Global firms in 2020…*). HCNs are citizens of the host country employed on local terms and conditions by the corporation (Przytuła, 2014; Scullion, Collings, 2006). LOPATs are defined as expatriates, who, after completing a home country–based long-term assignment contract, transition to full local terms and conditions in the host country, either as directed by the employer or at their own request (McNulty, DeCieri, 2015; McNulty, 2013; Vance, McNulty, Paik, 2015).

3.3 Normative approach

The third approach to thinking about leadership in a global context is to focus on enduring personal skills and abilities that are thought to characterize effective global leaders. It is called the **normative approach**, in which it is assumed that certain sets of leader's traits and abilities are common to all managers regardless of where they are working (Winsborough, Hogan, 2014). But we can only consider certain, single and specific competencies defined as individual abilities or characteristics, which are activated by a worker together with personal, organizational, or environmental resources to cope successfully with specific work situations (Capaldo et al., 2006). It cannot be related to whole constructs or competency models because there are neither best nor universal competency models that can be successfully applied in all types of organizations. Therefore, this calls for a more situational approach in competency management (Kupczyk, Stor, 2017, p. 102).

Some authors also warn that the situational context works as a filter that enables or disables using one's own competencies (Filipowicz, 2016), and thus no competency models or profiles are free from contextual influences (Kupczyk, Stor, 2017). Capaldo defines competencies as situated, idiosyncratic constructs whose meaning is deeply influenced by organizational culture and by the unique way people make sense of their jobs (Capaldo et al., 2006).

Competency management is understood as a set of activities performed in an organization and oriented toward identification, acquirement, development, and maintenance of such employees' competencies that enable the company reach its strategic goals (Kupczyk, Stor, 2017, p. 98).

The author found the normative and competency-based approaches the most appropriate when describing expatriates. According to the Brookfield Report (2016), 74 % of expatriates in leadership positions possess specific skills to be a leader in the host culture.

Literature and research in expatriate management provide a rich catalog of expatriate competencies that are the predictors of a successful foreign mission. Below, based on a review of previous research and empirical studies, the increasing need for leadership competencies in global business is presented.

4 Leadership competencies – required most in global business

Leadership seems to be the key, strategic competence required from global managers. The competencies evaluated as having the most impact on managers' effectiveness in global business were leadership and integrity, as well as decision making and managing teams. The importance of the first two is much more prevalent when analyzing characteristics appraised as crucial for the role. More than half of respondents indicated either leadership or integrity as the most significant trait for a successful manager, which seemed to be quite a meaningful result (Chłodna, 2015, p. 56).

The challenge of leadership is urgent and growing in importance. In a Cartus survey, 82 % of respondents stated that management and leadership roles are primary business drivers of long-term assignments (Cartus, 2016 p. 7), and a Deloitte report showed that leadership and development were among the most important priorities (89 %) for companies (*Global Human Capital Trends 2015).*

When asked about the most important leadership development priorities in global organizations, survey respondents were crystal clear. "Developing leaders to drive strategic change" was the top priority, followed by "filling gaps in the leadership pipeline" and, in third place, "driving culture change". But only 17 % of respondents were confident they had the right leadership in place to deliver on strategic business priorities. The survey respondents said they perceive that 62 % of first-level leaders, 47 % of mid-level leaders, and 41 % of high-potential leaders do not actively drive strategic change in their organization; this means that, on average, half of the leaders below the senior executive level are perceived as inactive in organizations' efforts to make strategic change (*Real World*, 2016, p. 7).

In another study, 89 % of executives rated the need to strengthen, reengineer, and improve "organizational leadership" as an important priority. The traditional pyramid-shaped leadership development model is simply not producing leaders fast enough to keep up with the demands of business and the pace of change. More than half of surveyed executives (56 %) report their companies are not ready to meet leadership needs. While investment in leadership development has grown by 10 % since 2015, progress has been disproportional. In fact, more than one in five companies (21 %) lack leadership programs altogether. Research findings suggest that organizations need to raise the bar in terms of rigor, evidence, and more structured and scientific approaches to identifying, assessing, and developing leaders, and that this process needs to start earlier in leaders' careers (*Global Human Capital Trends*, 2016). Multicultural sensitivity training represents one of the biggest opportunities to develop globally competent leaders, but in one study 44 % of organizations report that they offer global leadership development, and only 21 % see these programs as effective to a high or very high degree (Marin, 2014).

5 Expatriate leader's competencies – research review

An expatriate in a managerial position can also be seen as a global leader. Successful expatriate assignments are vital for developing global leaders (Cerdin et al., 2014; Zhang, 2012). A critical challenge for global firms is to implement assessment tools to develop expatriate leaders who can effectively manage role relationships across different directions in cross-national contexts (Kossek et al., 2017).

Global competence involves three interdependent dimensions. The first entails having a positive disposition toward cultural differences, requiring a sense of identity and self-esteem as well as empathy towards others. The second dimension is the ability to speak, understand, and think in languages beyond the language dominant in one's home country. Finally, global competence requires deep understanding of world history, geography, and a range of other key topics, like health, climate, and economics, and the capacity to think critically about current global challenges (Reimers, 2009).

Tab. 3 shows the key competences required from expatriate leaders, which are the result of a review of current research findings in the literature of "global leadership" and "expatriate management".

Wordle created the most frequent words from the above key competencies of a global expatriate (Fig. 5).

In the review of 20 years of research on global leadership competencies, M. Mendenhall and A. Bird found more than 150 different competencies that researchers had identified as being influential for global leadership success. Taking into account overlapping definitions and slight semantic differences, they were able to winnow this lengthy list down to 15 dimensions and group them into 6 broad categories. The competency categories are: traits and attitudes, cognitive orientations, intercultural relationships, global business expertise, global organizing expertise, and visioning. These six categories, in turn, can be grouped into two broad classes that we label **technical and social** competencies (Mendenhall, Bird, 2013).

Recent work on the **global mindset** (Javidan, Walker, 2013; Mendenhall et al., 2008) and **cultural intelligence** (Earley, Ang, 2003) illustrate this approach. For example, successful global leaders are thought by some to exhibit cosmopolitanism, cognitive complexity, mental inquisitiveness, honesty, humility, and personal resiliency. Leaders who possess this cluster of skills and abilities are thought to be prepared to manage effectively throughout much of the world (Steers et al., 2012).

Tab. 3: Key competencies of expatriate leaders. Source: own work based on literature review

Competencies	*Author*
Technical (predicated primarily on knowledge and the application of concepts, models, and techniques that can be learned and applied), e.g., global business expertise	(Mendenhall, Bird, 2013)
Social competencies (competencies related to traits and attitudes, cognitive orientations, and intercultural relationships entailing capabilities that are more difficult to teach and measure, and are centered more on human interaction), e.g., inquisitiveness, communication, creation and maintenance of trust across multiple relationships, integrity, humility, cognitive complexity, **cosmopolitanism**, **global mindset**, building community, ethics	(Mendenhall, Bird, 2013)
Global mindset (tolerance, flexibility, curiosity, and the ability to deal with uncertainty) (Briscoe, 2007); global mindset includes three capitals: global intellectual capital, global psychological capital, and global social capital Cultural intelligence	(Briscoe, 2007) (Javidan, Walker, 2013) (Earley, Ang, 2003)
Openness, extraversion, and emotional stability	(Caligiuri, 2013)
Sociability, emotional intelligence, optimism, self-confidence, conscientiousness, reconciliation, ESTJ personality	(Przytuła, 2014)
Cosmopolitanism, cognitive complexity, mental inquisitiveness, honesty, humility, and personal resiliency	(Steers et al., 2012)
Cross-cultural competence	(Magala, 2011; Rozkwitalska, 2011)
International experience, working in international context	(Brookfield, 2016; Davies et al., 2011)
Networking	(Durepos et al., 2012; Richardson, McKenna, 2014)
(Cultural) flexibility	(Przytuła, 2013b)(Cartus, 2016)
External awareness and appreciation of trends, visioning and strategy formulation, risk awareness, assessment and management, stakeholder engagement, flexibility and adaptability to change, ethics, and integrity	(*BSR Sustainability and Leadership Competencies for Business Leaders*, 2012)
Sense-making, social intelligence, novel and adaptive thinking, cross-cultural competency, computational thinking, new-media literacy, transdisciplinarity, design mindset, cognitive load management, virtual collaboration	(Davies, Fidler, 2011)

(*continued on next page*)

Tab. 3: (continued)

Competencies	*Author*
Ability to collaborate across boundaries, conceptualize new solutions, motivate diverse teams, and develop the next generation of diverse and global leaders	(*Global Human Capital Trends* 2016)
Strategic thinking, being inspirational, strong interpersonal skills, vision, passion and enthusiasm, decisiveness	(*The 2016 Deloitte Millennial Survey Winning over the next generation of leaders*, 2016)
Altrocentric[a], leaders-adaptable, flexible, multilingual, internationally mobile, with deep integrity and strong conceptual and strategic thinking skills, highly collaborative	(Hay Group, 2011)
Positive self-image, empathy, interest in local culture, tolerance for ambiguity, flexibility, initiative, sociability, open-mindedness	(Grovewell: Global Leadership Solution, 2017)
Multicultural sensitivity, awareness, the ability to communicate effectively, strategic thinking, ethics, integrity	(*UNC Leadership Survey 2015*)

[a] Altrocentric is the opposite of egocentric (ego meaning self in Latin, alter meaning the other). The defining attribute of altrocentric leaders is a focus on and concern for others rather than themselves.

According to P. Caligiuri, effective and culturally agile global leaders know that while there are times when cultural adaptation is needed, there are also times when cultural adaptability is inappropriate, when the best approach is to minimize the differences across cultures and maintain the organization's standard. There are three personality traits responsible for performing the most appropriate approach: **openness, extraversion,** and **emotional stability**. Leaders with higher levels of these personality characteristics are more likely to interact with others from different cultures, seek novel cross-cultural experiences, and act with resilience in ambiguous situations often encountered when working internationally (Caligiuri, 2013, p. 178).

S. Przytuła also pointed out the psychological traits which are positively correlated with a successful expatriate mission, for example: sociability, emotional intelligence, optimism, self-confidence, conscientiousness, reconciliation, and ESTJ personality (Przytuła, 2014, p. 122).

Cross-cultural competence is the individual's ability to make effective use of knowledge, skills, and personal qualities in achieving success, in working with people of different cultures. It consists of personality traits, knowledge of the culture, and ability to apply knowledge in action (Rozkwitalska, 2011, p. 94).

Fig. 6: Word cloud for expat leader's competencies. Source: www.wordle.net.

According to S. Magala (2011), "it's a backpack or a set of tools that all learners are picking up when they have to deal with a variety of cultural software in one place. They learn because they have to move among different cultures and subcultures".

Due to the "content" of cultural competence, it can be said that it is rather "metacompetence", because it contains many features, psychophysical properties, elements of knowledge, experience, and skills, which enable the expatriate to function and act in conditions of great cultural diversity (Przytuła, 2014, p. 120).

Research on predicted key competencies for global leaders in the next decade shows that 93 % of employers believe that **international experience** and intercultural work will be crucial, and 89 % of respondents pointed to mobility and language skills (Davies et al., 2011). According to a Global Relocation Trends Report (Brookfield, 2016), 61 % of the survey respondents say their company has communicated to employees that taking an international assignment is important to optimize their careers. Huang et al. (2005) strongly suggested that prior international experience is significantly and positively correlated with adjustment to foreign culture.

According to some researchers, networking will also be demanding, defined as "the ability to search, establish and maintain interpersonal relationships internationally", which is explained by the "actor network theory" (Durepos, Mills, 2012), or "social network theory" (Richardson, McKenna, 2014).

Cultural flexibility is defined as cognitive openness to cultural diversity, willingness to experiment with other customs and ways of living than one's own, and an

high national identity	**ethnocentrics**	**internationalist**
low national identity	**transitionalist**	**transnationalist**
	low cross border business focus	high cross border business focus

Fig. 7: Types of cross-border managers. Source: Cogin, Fish (2010).

ability to adapt to changes in culturally diverse environments (Przytuła, 2013b). In a Cartus study, 76 % of survey respondents report an increase in the need for **flexibility** in their mobility programs (Cartus, 2016).

A research survey by J. Cogin and A. Fish based on 658 managers presents the typology of four types of cross-border managers, due to two dimensions: national identity and cross-cultural business focus (Fig. 7).

One dimension of the taxonomy – "national identity" – was defined as: the influence a manager's values might have on their social behavior when they encounter a new environment, and as a result, the extent to which inappropriate values might compromise behavior and ultimately cross-cultural effectiveness. A strong national identity creates a blockade ("cultural security"), which prevents adaptation to different cultural conditions. The other dimension – "cross-cultural business focus" – was defined as: behavior that seeks out and values culturally diverse business situations and learns from these differences.

Transnationalists[1] – an individual who is high on "a cross-border business focus" and low on "national identity". A Transnationalist is someone who is essentially a multiculturalist; one who tends not to value any given culture over and above another, and one who has the ability to move and adapt quite easily between cultures and seek out opportunities to develop and learn from cultural differences.

Internationalists – a person who is high on both dimensions. Internationalists are likely to value a cross-border management role and the opportunities it

1 In research, as many as 78 % of transnationalists had prior international experience as a result of their earlier travel abroad, and 71 % knew one more foreign language besides English, which proves their willingness to learn (Cogin, Fish, 2010).

brings, however would believe in home country superiority with respect to social differences.

Transitionalists – those who are low on both dimensions. While not believing one culture is superior to another, a Transitionalist does not see advantages in seeking out multiple cultural views and learning from differences. A Transitionalist may fail to see advantages in extending their career reach to somewhere different, particularly a foreign location.

Ethnocentrics – those who are low on "a cross-border business focus" and high on "national identity". An Ethnocentric highly values their own cultural identity and may regard it as superior to others. In a cross-border role, an Ethnocentric may have considerable difficulty coming to terms with cultural differences and ultimately adjusting to the experience.

The results highlight that the most appropriate cross-border manager type appears to be the Transnationalist, and, importantly for all types of cross-border assignments, not simply the medium- to long-term assignment that demands significant social and business adjustment abilities. This type appeals to the argument from Foulkes (1995) that such individuals are not simply, "rounded in their own culture but have the culture-general and culture-specific skills to be able to live, interact and work effectively in a multicultural environment". This supports also a concept of "effective multi-culturalist functioning by the cosmopolitan planetary citizen, namely, the Transcultural leader" (Foulkes, 1995).

Another list of the top competencies of global leaders was identified in a **BSR Report** (2012, p. 6), which were: external awareness and appreciation of trends, visioning and strategy formulation, risk awareness, assessment and management stakeholder engagement, flexibility and adaptability to change, ethics, and integrity.

The authors of *Future Work Skills 2020 Report* (Davies, Fidler, 2011) listed the most important competencies for global leaders in XXI century:

- Sense-making: the ability to determine the deeper meaning or significance of what is being expressed;
- Social intelligence: the ability to connect to others in a deep and direct way, to sense and stimulate reactions and desired interactions;
- Novel and adaptive thinking: proficiency at thinking and coming up with solutions and responses beyond that which is rote or rule-based;
- Cross-cultural competency: the ability to operate in different cultural settings;
- Computational thinking: the ability to translate vast amounts of data into abstract concepts and to understand data-based reasoning;

- New-media literacy: the ability to critically assess and develop content that uses new media forms, and to leverage these media for persuasive communication;
- Transdisciplinarity: literacy in and ability to understand concepts across multiple disciplines;
- Design mindset: the ability to represent and develop tasks and work processes for desired outcomes;
- Cognitive load management: the ability to discriminate and filter information for importance, and to understand how to maximize cognitive functioning using a variety of tools and techniques;
- Virtual collaboration: the ability to work productively, drive engagement, and demonstrate presence as a member of a virtual team.

Some other researchers noticed the importance of finding ways to develop leaders who can collaborate extensively and focus on new leadership cohorts (e.g., millennials, women, and diverse individuals). Surprisingly, 59 % of respondents to our survey report "little" to "no investment" in diverse leaders, with similar findings for millennials (59 %) and women (49 %). Such investments, however, are extremely important to allow companies to leverage the strengths of millennial leaders – often well suited to rapid learning and conceptual thinking – and baby boomer leaders in their 50s and 60s – who often bring strengths in behavior and influence along with valuable institutional knowledge.

The challenge is to combine and build the strengths of leaders at all levels and of all descriptions. A millennial leadership style is "socially focused", so a new millennial leader should display these personality traits: strategic thinking (39 %), being inspirational (37 %), strong interpersonal skills (34 %), vision (31 %), passion and enthusiasm (30 %), and decisiveness (30 %) (*The 2016 Deloitte Millennial*, 2016, p. 4).

According to a **Grovewell report** (2017), the managerial qualities that correlate with success in a different environment and culture include: positive self-image, empathy, interest in local culture, tolerance for ambiguity, flexibility, initiative, sociability, and open-mindedness.

Conclusions and future directions

- The demand is growing for globally minded, culturally sophisticated leaders who can produce results on the world stage, regardless of nationality.
- Expatriate assignments are vital for developing global leaders.
- The expatriate leadership is based on the unique existing competency configuration of manager and positional requirements.

- Leadership is a cultural construct.
- To make matters even more complex, not only does the term "leader" translate differently across various cultural groups, but also the meanings that are construed from these translations can also differ, sometimes significantly. For example, in individualistic societies leadership typically refers to a single person who takes charge and leads the organization to targeted performance. In collectivistic societies leadership is more aligned with group endeavors.
- Expatriate managers work with host-country nationals in many cultural settings, a growing number of which may have very dissimilar values on leadership and employment relation.
- More research is needed to increase the understanding of the assessment and development of expatriates' leadership effectiveness amid a context of divergent cultural expectations.

It can be said that no matter where an organization is located, and what their growth goals may be, the majority recognize that enhancing the global competence of their leaders will result in significant advantages (*UNC Leadership Survey, 2015*).

The success of foreign assignments depends, among others, on good, positive adaptation to new work, and the social and cultural environment. The positive attitude of expatriate leaders may bring in positive results not only from an individual perspective (e.g., compassion, satisfaction, sense of accomplishment, development mastery, well-being) but also from a group perspective (e.g., creativity, group effectiveness, synergy, well-being of the group members), and furthermore they are the strengths of the organization (Youssef, Luthans, 2012; Przytuła et al., 2014).

References

Agrawal, A., Rook, C. (2014). Global leaders in east and west: Do all global leaders lead in the same way? In Y. Osland, J. S., Li, M., Wang (Ed.), *Advances in Global Leadership*. Bingley: Emerald. 231–240.

Al Ariss, A., Crowley-Henry, M. (2013). Self-initiated expatriation and migration in the management literature: Present theorizations and future research directions. *Career Development International*, *18*(1), 78–96. http://doi.org/10.1108/13620431311305962.

Andresen, M., Bergdolt, F., Margenfeld, J., Dickmann, M. (2014). Addressing international mobility confusion-developing definitions and differentiations for self-initiated and assigned expatriates as well as migrants. *The International Journal of Human Resource Management*, *25*, 2295–2318.

Arasaratnam, L. A. (2013). A review of articles on multiculturalism in 35 years of IJIR. *International Journal of Intercultural Relations, 37*(6), 676–685.

Avolio, B., Luthans, F. (2006). In F. Avolio, B. Luthans (Ed.), *The High Impact Leader: Moments Matter in Accelerating Authentic Leadership Development*. New York: McGraw Hill. 83–87.

Aycan, Z. (2008). Cross-cultural approaches to leadership. In D. Smith, P. Peterson, M. Thomas (Ed.), *Cross-Cultural Management Research* (pp. 219–238). New York: Sage Publications.

Aycan, Z., Kanungo, R., Yu, C., Deller, J, Stahl, G., Kurshid, A. (2000). Impact of culture on human resources management practices:10 countries comparison. *Applied Psychology An International Review*, *49*(1), 192–221.

Bass, B. M. (1990). Leadership in different countries and cultures. In S. Bass (Ed.), *Handbook of Leadership*. New York: Free Press.

Beechler, S., Baltzley, D. (2008). Creating a global mindset. *Chief Learning Officer*, June, 40–45.

Black, J. S., Porter, L. W. (1991). Managerial behaviors and job performance: A successful manager in Los Angeles may not succeed in Hong Kong. *Journal of International Business Studies, 22*(1), 99–113.

Bolden, R., Gosling, J., Marturano, A. and Dennison, P. (2003). *A Review of Leadership Theory and Competency Frameworks*. Exeter: Centre for Leadership Studies.

Brake, T. (1997). *The Global Leader-Critical Factors for Creating the World Class Organization*. Chicago: Irwin.

Brewster, C. (1991). *The Management of Expatriates*. London: Kogan Page.

Briscoe, D. (2007). Developing a global mindset: its role in global careers. In R. O. P. Benson, A. Mahajan, R. Alas (Ed.), *The 9th International Human Resource Management Conference, Conference Proceedings*. Talinn: NMSU College of Business.

Brookfield Global Relocation Trends. (2016). *Global Mobility Trends Survey*. New York: BGRS.

Caligiuri, P. (2006). Developing global leaders. *Human Resource Management Review*, *16*, 219–228.

Caligiuri, P. (2013). Developing culturally agile global business leaders. *Organizational Dynamics*, *42*, 175–182.

Caligiuri, P., Tarique, L. (2009). Predicting effectiveness in global leadership activities. *Journal of World Business*, *44*, 336–346.

Caliuri P. M. (2000). The big five personality characteristics as predictors of expatriates desire to terminate the assignment and supervisor-rated performance. *Personnel Psychology*, *53*, 67–88.

Capaldo, G., Iandoli, L., Zollo, G. (2006). A situationalist perspective to competency management. *Human Resources Management*, *45*(3), 429–448.

Cartus. (2016). *Trends in global relocation. Global mobility policy & practices survey report*. Danburry, CT: Cartus Corporation.

Cerdin, J. L., Brewster, C. (2014). Talent management and expatriation: bridging two streams of research and practice. *Journal of World Business*, *49*, 245–252.

Chłodna, J. (2015). Righteous non-charismatic leader most effective in Polish organizations? In search of a culture sensitive competency model for Poland. *Humanities and Social Sciences*, *22*(4), 45–62.

Clapp-Smith, R., Lester, G. V. (2014). Defining the "mindset" in global mindset: Modelling the dualities of global leadership. *Advances in Global Leadership*, *8*, 205–228.

Cogin J., Fish, A. (2010). Modelling and predicting the performance of cross border managers. *Personnel Review*, *39*(4). 432-447

Collins Dictionaries (2011).https://www.collinsdictionary.com. Accessed 2 January 2019.

Dabic, M., Gonzalez-Loureiro, M., Harvey, M. (2013). Evolving research on expatriates (1970–2012). *International Journal of Human Resource Management*, *26*(3), 316–337.

Davies, A., Fidler, D., Gorbis, M. (2011). *Future Work Skills 2020*. Phoenix.

Dessler, G. (2003). In G. Dessler (ed.), *Human Resource Management*. New Jersey: Prentice Hall.

Doherty, N., Richardson, J., Thorn, K. (2013). Self-initiated expatriation and self-initiated expatriates: Clarification of the research stream. *Career Development International*, *18*(1), 97–112. http://doi.org/10.1108/13620431311305971

Dorfman, P., Javidan, M., Hanges, P. J., Dastmalchian, A., House, R. (2012). GLOBE: A twenty year journey into the intriguing world of culture and leadership. *Journal of World Business*, *47*, 504–518.

Dowling P., Festing, M. E. A. (2008). *International Human Resource Management*. South-New York: Western Cengage Learning.

Durepos, G, Mills, A. J. (2012). *ANTi-History: Theorizing in Past, History and Historiography, Information*. Charlotte, NC: Age Publishing.

Dziatzko, N., Struve, F., Stehr, C. (2016). Global leadership: How to lead Multicultural Teams effectively? *Journal of Intercultural Management (in printing)*.

Earley, P., Ang, S. (2003). In S. Earley, P., Ang (Ed.), *Cultural Intelligence: Individual Interactions across Cultures*. Palo Alto: Stanford University Press.

Engelen, A., Schmidt, S., Strenger, L., Brettel, M. (2014). Top management's transformational leader behaviors and innovation orientation: A cross-cultural perspective in eight countries. *Journal of Intercultural Management, 20*, 124–136.

Filipowicz, G. (2016). *Zarządzanie kompetencjami. Perspektywa firmowa i osobista*. Warszawa: Oficyna Wolters Kluwer.

Forster, N. (2000). The myth of the "international manager." *International Journal of Human Resource Management, 11*(1), 605–623.

Foulkes, R. A. (1995). Globalising organisations and empowering people for high-performance leadership of our multicultural world: or behold, the demise of business-as-usual is at hand. *Equal Opportunities International, 14*(1/2), 37–46.

Fry, L. (2003). Toward a theory of spiritual leadership. *The Leadership Quarterly, 14*, 693–727.

Ghemawat, P. (2012). Developing Global Leaders. *Mc Kinsey Quarterly*. Retrieved from http://www.mckinsey.com/global-themes/leadership/developing-global-leaders?cid=eml-web. Accessed 12 December 2018.

Global Human Capital Trends 2015. Leading in the new world of work. (2015). London: Deloitte University Press.

Global Human Capital Trends. The new organization: Different by design. (2016). London: Deloitte University Press.

Green, N. (2009). Expatriation, expatriates and expats. The American transformation of a concept. *American Historican Review, April*.

Grovewell: Global Leadership Solution. (2017). Expatriate Competencies. Retrieved from https://www.grovewell.com/expatriate-competence/. Accessed 14 August 2018.

Hanges, P. J., Aiken J., Park, J., Su, J. (2016). Cross-cultural leadership: Leading around the world. *Current Opinion in Psychology, 8*, 64–69.

Haromszeki, Ł. (2014). Expectations towards Global Organisational Leaders. *Zeszyty Naukowe UE W Krakowie, 9*(933), 109–122.

Harzing, A. W. (2004). Composing an International Staff. In A. W. Harzing (Ed.), *International Human Resources Management* (pp. 252–266). London & Thousand Oaks: Sage Publications.

Hay Group. (2011). *Building the new leader. Leadership challenges of the future revealed*. New York: HayGroup Leadership Whitepaper.

Hippler, T., Haslberger, A., Brewster, C. (2017). Expatriate adjustment. In J. McNulty, Y., Selmer (Ed.), *Research Handbook of Expatriates* (pp. 83–105). Cheltenham: Edward Elgar Publishing.

Huang, T., Chi, S., Lawler, J. (2005). The relationship between expatriates' personality traits and their adjustment to international assignments. *International Journal of HRM, 16*(9). 1656–1670.

International Organization for Migration (IOM). (2016). *World Migration 2016*. Geneva.

Javidan, M., Walker, J. (2013). *Developing Your Global Mindset*. (J. Javidan, M., Walker, Ed.). Edina: Beaver's Pond Press.

Kawczyńska-Butrym, Z. (2017). Mobilność i decyzje migracyjne-uwarunkowania i aktorzy. In S. Przytuła (Ed.), *Migracje międzynarodowe i ekspatriacja.Perspektywa indywidualna, organizacyjna, społeczno-kulturowa*. Warszawa: Difin.

Kossek, E., Huang, J., Piszczek, P., Fleenor, J., Ruderman, M. (2017). Rating expatriate leader effectiveness in multisource feedback systems: Cultural distance and hierarchical effects. *Human Resource Management*, *56*(1), 151–172.

Kraimer, M., Bolino, M., Mead, B. (2016). Themes in expatriate and repatriate research over four decades: What do we know and what do we still need to learn? *Annual Review of Organizational Psychology and Organizational Behavior*, *3*(1), 1–27.

Kupczyk, T., Stor, M. (2017). In M. Kupczyk, T., Stor (Ed.), *Competency Management. Theory, Research and Business Practice*. Warsaw: University of Business in Wroclaw.

Lauring, J., Selmer, J. (2012). International language management and diversity climate in multicultural organizations. *International Business Review*, *21*(2), 156–166.

Lauring, J., Selmer, J. (2011). Multicultural organizations: Common language, knowledge sharing and performance. *Personnel Review*, *40*(3), 324–343. http://doi.org/10.1108/00483481111118649.

Lawson, K.S., Swain, P. A. (1985). Leadership style: Differences between expatriates and locals. *Leadership and Organization Development Journal*, *6*(4), 8–11.

Magala, S. (2011). *Kompetencje międzykulturowe*. Warsaw: Oficyna a Wolters Kluwer business.

Marin, K. (2014). How to build global leaders. *Chief Learning Officer*. Retrieved from http://www.clomedia.com/articles/6010-how-to-build-global-leaders.

Martin, G., Resick, C., Keating, M., Dickson, M. (2009). Ethical leadership across cultures. A comparative analysis of German and US perspective. *Business Ethics: A European Review*, *18*(2), 127–144.

Mączyński, J., Sułkowski, Ł. (2017). A seven nation study of leadership attributes. *Polish Psychological Bulletin*, *48*(2), 307–314.

McCall, M., Hollenbeck, J. (2002). *Developing Global Executives. The Lessons of International Experience*. Boston: Harvard Business School Press.

McNulty, I. (2013). Are self-initiated expatriates born or made? Exploring the relationship between SIE orientation and individual ROI. In A. Vaiman, V., Haslberger (Ed.), *Talent Management of Self-Initiated expatriates* (pp. 30–58). London: Palgrave Macmillan.

McNulty, I., Brewster, C. (2017). The concept of business expatriates. In J. McNulty, I., Selmer (Ed.), *Research Handbook of Expatriates* (pp. 21–55). London: Elgar Publishing.

McNulty, I., DeCieri, H. (2015). Linking global mobility and global talent management: The role of ROI. *Employee Relations*, *38*(1), 8–30.

McNulty, Y., Brewster, C. (2017). Theorizing the meaning(s) of "expatriate": Establishing boundary conditions for business expatriates. *The International Journal of Human Resource Management*, *28*(1), 27–61.

McNulty, Y., Selmer, J. (2017). Introduction: overview of early expatriate studies, 1952 to 1979. In J. McNulty, Y., Selmer (Ed.), *Research Handbook of Expatriates* (pp. 3–20). London: Elgar Publishing.

McPhail, R., Fisher, M., Harvey, M., Moeller, M. (2012). Staffing the global organization: Cultural nomads. *Human Resource Development Quarterly*, *23*(2), 259–276.

Mendenhall, M., Bird, A. (2013). In search of global leadership. *Organizational Dynamics*, *42*, 167–174.

Mendenhall, M., Oddou, G., Osland, J., Bird, A., Maznevski, M. (2008). In M. Mendenhall, M., Oddou, G., Osland, J., Bird, A., Maznevski Ed.), *Global Leadership. Research, Practice and Development*. London: Routledge.

Mendenhall, M., Reiche S., Bird, A., Osland, J. S. (2012). Defining the " 'global' " in global leadership. *Journal of World Business*, *47*, 493–503.

Molloy, J., Ployhart, R. (2012). Construct clarity: Multidisciplinary considerations and an illustration using human capital. *Human Resource Management Review*, *22*, 152–156.

Oxford Dictionary of English (2015). https://en.oxforddictionaries.com. Accessed: 27 March 2018.

Osland, J. (2008). Overview of the global leadership literature. In M. Mendenhall, M., Oddou, G., Osland, J., Bird, A., Maznevski (Ed.), *Global Leadership Research, Practice and Development*. London: Routledge.

Osland, J. S., Bird, A., Mendenhall M. (2012). The context of expert global leadership. *Advances in Global Leadership*, *7*, 227–259.

Osland, J. S, Ehret, M., Ruiz, L. (2017). Case studies of global leadership: Expert cognition in the domain of large-scale global change. *Advances in Global Leadership*, 10, 41–88.

Przytuła, S. (2013a). Expatriate manager-who is it? An attempt of term explication and outline of definition. In *Conference Proceedings "International Management."* Berlin: EIASM-ESCP Europe, 45-61.

Przytuła, S. (2013b). Flexibility - as a feature and the ability in the expatriate' qualification profile. *Education of Economists and Managers, 27*, 51–65.

Przytuła, S. (2014). *Zarządzanie kadrą ekspatriantów w filiach przedsiębiorstw międzynarodowych w Polsce*. Warszawa: CeDeWu.

Przytuła, S. (2015). Migrants, Assigned Expatriates (AE) and Self-initiated Expatriates (SIE) - Differentiation of terms and literature-based research review. *Journal of Intercultural Management, 7*(2), 89–112.

Przytuła, S. (2016). Self-initiated expatriation (SIE) as the form of international employees' mobility. *Human Resource Management, 6*(113), 75–92.

Przytuła, S., Rozkwitalska, M., Chmielecki, M., Sułkowski, Ł. (2014). Cross-cultural interactions between expatriates and local managers in the light of positive organizational scholarship-practice from Poland. *Social Sciences, 4*(86),14-24.

Przytuła, S., Rozkwitalska, M., Chmielecki, M., Sułkowski, Ł., & Basinska, B. A. (2014). Cross-cultural interactions between expatriates and local managers in the light of Positive Organizational Behaviour. *Social Sciences (Socialiniai Mokslai), 4*(4), 14–24. http://doi.org/10.5755/j01.ss.86.4.9261.

Real World Leadership Develop leaders who can drive real change. (2016). London: Korn Ferry Institute.

Reimers, F. M. (2009). Global competency. *Harvard International Review, 30*(4), 24–27.

Report BSR Sustainability and Leadership Competencies for Business Leaders. (2012). Retrieved from https://www.bsr.org/reports/BSR_Sustainability_Leadership_Competencies.pdf.

Richardson, J., McKenna, S. (2014). Towards an understanding of social networks among organizational self-initiated expatriates: A qualitative case study of a professional services firm. *International Journal of Human Resource Management, 25*(19), 2627–2643.

Rodsutti, M., Swierczek, F.W. (2002). Leadership and organizational effectiveness in multinational enterprises in southest Asia. *Leadership and Organization Development Journal, 23*(5), 250–259.

Rogers, E., Blonski, D. (2010). The global leadership mindset. *Chief Learning Officer*, June, 19–21.

Rozkwitalska, M. (2011). *Bariery w zarządzaniu międzykulturowym. Perspektywa filii zagranicznych korporacji transnarodowych*. Warsaw: Oficyna a Wolters Kluwer business.

Rozkwitalska, M., Sułkowski, Ł. (Ed.). (2016). *Współpraca zawodowa w środowisku wielokulturowym*. Warszawa: Wolters Kluwer Polska.

Scheffer, J., Werner, H. (2012). Widerstände der Vernetzung. Interkulturelle Kommunikation in virtuellen Teams am Beispiel deutsch-amerikanischer Arbeitsgruppen bei der BMW Group. In Reutner U. (Ed.), *Von der digitalen zur interkulturellen Revolution*. Baden-Baden: Nomos Verlag.

Scullion, H., Collings, D. (2006). *Global staffing*. New York, London: Routledge.

Selmer, J. (1995). *Expatriate Management. New Ideas for International Business*. (J. Selmer, Ed.). Westport: Quorum Books.

Selmer, J. (1996). Expatriate or local bosses? HCN subordinates' preferences in leadership behaviour. *The International Journal of Human Resources Management*, *7*(1), 160–166.

Smith, P. B., Misumi, J, Tayeb, M., Peterson, M. and Bond, M. (1989). On the generality of leadership style measures across cultures. *Journal of Occupational Psychology*, *62*, 97–109.

Spreitzer, G. M., McCall., M., Mahoney, W. (1997). The early identification of international executive potential. *Journal of Applied Psychology*, *82*(1), 6–29.

Steers, R., Sanchez-Runde, C., Nardon, L. (2012). Leadership in a global context: New directions in research and theory development. *Journal of World Business*, *47*, 479–482.

Stening, B. W., Hammer, M. R. (1992). Cultural baggage and the adaptation of expatriate American and Japanese managers'. *Management International Review*, *1*, 77–89.

Suutari, V. (2002). Global leader development: An emerging research agenda. *Career Development International*, *7*(4), 218–233.

Suutari, V., Brewster, C. (2009). Beyond expatriation: Different forms of international employment. In P. Sparrow (Ed.), *Handbook of International Human Resource Management: Integrating People, Process and Context* (pp. 131–150). Chichester.

Suutari, V., Tornikoski C., Makela, L. (2012). Career decision making of global careerists. *Journal of Human Resource Management*, *23*(15–16), 3455–3478.

Takahashi, K., Ishikawa, J., Kanai, T. (2012). Qualitative and quantitative studies of leadership in multinational settings: Meta-analytic and cross-cultural reviews. *Journal of World Business*, *47*, 530–538.

Tharenou, P. (2013). Self-initiated expatriate: An alternative to company assigned expatriates? *Journal of Global Mobility*, *1*(3), 336–356.

Tharenou, P. (2017). Methodological issues in expatriate studies and future directions. In J. McNulty, Y., Selmer (Ed.), *Research handbook of expatriates* (pp. 393–415). London: Elgar Publishing.

Tharenou, P., & Caulfield, N. (2010). Will I stay or will I go? Explaining repatriation by self-initiated expatriates. *Academy of Management Journal*, *53*(5), 1009–1028. http://doi.org/10.5465/AMJ.2010.54533183.

The 2016 Deloitte Millennial Survey Winning over the next generation of leaders. (2016). Retrieved from www.deloitte.com/MillennialSurvey

The United Nations. (2015). *International Migration Report 2015.*

Tung, R. (2016). New perspectives on human resource management in a global context. *Journal of World Business*, *51*, 142–152.

UNC Leadership Survey 2015 Compete and Connect: Developing Globally-Competent Leaders. (2015).

Vance, C., McNulty, I., Paik, Y. (2015). *The Expat-preneur: A Growing Career Phenomenon for the Global Market Place.* Kauai.

Vertovec, S. (2006). *The Emergence of Super-Diversity in Britain.* Oxford.

Winsborough, D., Hogan, R. (2014). Evaluating global leadership: Does culture matter? *Advances in Global Leadership*, *8*, 45–65.

Ya Ping, C. (2009). Influence on expatriate social networks in China. *The International Journal of HRM*, *20*(4), 790–809.

Youssef, C. M. and Luthans, F. (2012). Positive global leadership. *Journal of World Business*, *47*(4), 539–547.

Zhang, Y. (2012). Expatriate development for cross-cultural adjustment. Effects of cultural distance and cultural intelligence. *Human Resource Development Review*, *12*(2), 177–199.

Jerzy Mączyński and Łukasz Sułkowski

A Seven-Nation Study of Leadership Attributes

Abstract: *The overall purpose of this chapter was to compare a representative sample of Polish middle managers with a representative sample of chief executive officers (CEOs) from six chosen countries, in regard to selected leadership traits and behaviors. We present a small portion of data collected under the GLOBE project, Phase 3, and longitudinal research findings concerning subordinates' assessments of Polish middle managers in relation to their attributes from 2008 to 2012. The GLOBE, Phase 3 research is the first study to investigate several thousands of CEOs and senior management teams in 24 countries, to empirically and directly assess the relationship between culture and leadership traits and behaviors. We provide research evidence that the investigated CEOs from the United States, Austria, Germany, China, and Taiwan (with the exception of Russian CEOs and Polish middle managers) were generally positively evaluated by their direct staff in regard to: inspirational, visionary, integrity, and performance-oriented leadership behaviors (constituents of charismatic leadership), team-oriented behavior, and participative leadership style. Empirical findings under the GLOBE project, Phase 3 revealed that the charismatic leadership behavior of CEOs has a huge influence on top management teams' (TMTs) dedication to organizational goals, and is the most predictive of all leadership behaviors for TMT commitment to organizations. The analyzed research findings indicate that CEOs in Russia and Polish middle managers display strong similarities. They tend to behave in less charismatic, team-oriented, and participative ways than CEOs in the remaining countries.*

Keywords: Leader attributes, charismatic leadership, dedication to organizational goals

Note: This chapter was previously published in the Polish Psychological Bulletin, 217, Vol. 48 (2), 307–314.

Introduction

Our chapter focuses on the findings from the GLOBE project, Phase 3 and middle Polish managers concerning leadership traits and behaviors. A significant part of our chapter focuses on the relationships between traits and behaviors of Chief Executive Officers (CEOs) and Top Management Teams' (TMTs) dedication to organizational goals. In our chapter we present a small portion of the data collected under the GLOBE project, Phase 3[1], and longitudinal research results concerning followers' evaluations of Polish middle managers in regard to their traits and behaviors in the years of 2008–2012.

Leadership in organizations has been a significant area of research over the last few decades. Both Bass (1990) and Yukl (1994) present a comprehensive review of the extensive literature on leadership developed over the years. Nevertheless one area in which new developments in leadership research are required is cross-cultural studies (House et al.; 2004, 2014; Smith et al., 1994, 1998; Sułkowski, 2012). The GLOBE project, intended to fill this gap, is an international research program developed by Robert House in 1993, which focuses on leadership perceptions of practices and leader attributes cross-culturally (House et al., 1997). In the GLOBE study, leadership is defined as "the ability of an individual to influence, motivate and enable others to contribute towards the effectiveness and success of the organization of which they are members" (Den Hartog et al., 1997, p. 256).

Phase 3 of the GLOBE project particularly examines the relationships between the observed leadership traits and behaviors of CEOs, and TMTs' dedication to work performance. In total, 24 countries participated in Phase 3. From this broad sample, we chose for our analyses six countries: Austria, Germany, and Russia from Europe; China and Taiwan from Asia; and the United States from North America. Poland did not participate in the GLOBE project, Phase 3, but nevertheless the authors of this chapter collected the data concerning followers' evaluations of Polish middle managers in regard to their traits and behaviors in the years of 2008–2012. A longitudinal study was conducted among 342 followers employed by over 300 organizations located in different parts of Poland (including Legnica, Świdnica, Wrocław, Łódź, Warszawa). Followers of Polish middle managers, tested in those years, completed identical questionnaires as followers investigated under the GLOBE project, Phase 3. Hypothesizing on the basis of extrapolation, the data collected among Polish middle managers can be compared with the data collected under the GLOBE project, Phase 3. Nevertheless, further research is required among a representative sample of Polish CEOs, in order to acquire strong empirical evidence that our hypothesis is valid.

Under the GLOBE project, Phase 3, the three following hypotheses were tested, assuming that CEOs' leadership behaviors predict TMT dedication and firm competitive performance:

---

1 More comprehensive analyses of the present study can be found in Robert J. House et al. (2014), "Strategic Leadership Across Cultures, The GLOBE Study of CEO Leadership Behavior and Effectiveness in 24 Countries." Sage Publications, Inc. 2014.

1. CEO charismatic leadership behavior will be positively associated with TMT dedication and firm competitive performance.
2. CEO team-oriented leadership behavior will be positively associated with TMT dedication and firm competitive performance.
3. CEO participative leadership behavior will be positively associated with TMT dedication and firm competitive performance.

In multilevel analysis, CEO leadership behavior served as the independent variable and TMT dedication and firm competitive performance as dependent variables.

1 Method

The leadership measurements surveyed followers of CEOs as well as Polish middle managers to assess their superiors according to six attributes that are presented below:

1. Performance Leadership Dimension: improvement-oriented, excellence-oriented, achievement-oriented.
2. Integrity Leadership Dimension: honest, sincere, just, trustworthy.
3. Visionary Leadership Dimension: foresight, prepared, anticipatory, plans ahead.
4. Inspirational Leadership Dimension: enthusiastic, positive, morale booster, motive arouser.
5. Team Orientation: group-oriented, collaborative, loyal, consultative.
6. Participative Leadership Dimension: involvement of subordinates in the decision-making process and implementation.

In generating leadership traits and behaviors, the items were based on several existing leadership theories, as described by House et al. [1997]. All scales developed in the GLOBE project are based on an extensive pilot study (see House et al., 2004). Questionnaire items developed in the GLOBE project were translated from English to Polish, and later translated back into English. The reverse translation was checked by the GLOBE coordinating team. Data were collected from the immediate subordinates of the CEOs (i.e., directly reporting subordinates and advisers). Three randomly selected TMT members (directly reporting to a respective CEO) were asked to complete the GLOBE project, Phase 3 survey questionnaire forms, developed to assess CEO traits and behaviors. A total of more than 1,000 CEOs and 5,000 of their direct staff (TMTs) were respondents in the GLOBE project, Phase 3.

Tab. 1: Rank order of selected CEO leadership behaviors predicting top management team dedication and firm competitive performance.

TMT Dedication		**Firm Competitive Performance**	
Leadership Behavior	Correlation	Leadership Behavior	Correlation
Inspirational Leadership Dimension	.36**	Visionary Leadership Dimension	.29**
Visionary Leadership Dimension	.35**	Team Integration	.26**
Integrity Leadership Dimension	.35**	Inspirational Leadership Dimension	.19**
Performance Leadership Dimension	.33**	Performance Leadership Dimension	.16*
Team Integration	.24**	Integrity Leadership Dimension	.16*
Participative Leadership Dimension	.22**		
Autocratic Leadership Dimension	-.12**		

N = 998 for TMT Dedication. N = 255 for Firm Competitive Performance.
*p < .05. **p < .01.

2 Research results

First of all in Tab. 1 we present selected key CEO leadership traits and behaviors predicting TMT dedication to organizational goals and firm competitive performance.

Research findings under the GLOBE project, Phase 3, presented in Tab. 1 indicate that inspirational, visionary, integrity, and performance leadership behaviors, as constituents of charismatic leadership, play a significant role in TMT dedication to organizational goals and firm competitive performance.

In addition, the data displayed in Tab. 1 indicate that participative CEO leadership was predictive of TMT dedication, but not firm competitive performance. Its predictive power for TMT dedication was less than that of charismatic leadership (inspirational, visionary, integrity, performance-oriented) and team-oriented leadership (House et al., 2014).

Research findings concerning cross-cultural studies in regard to leadership attributes (inspirational, visionary, integrity, performance-oriented, team-oriented, and participative leadership styles) are presented in the subsequent figures.

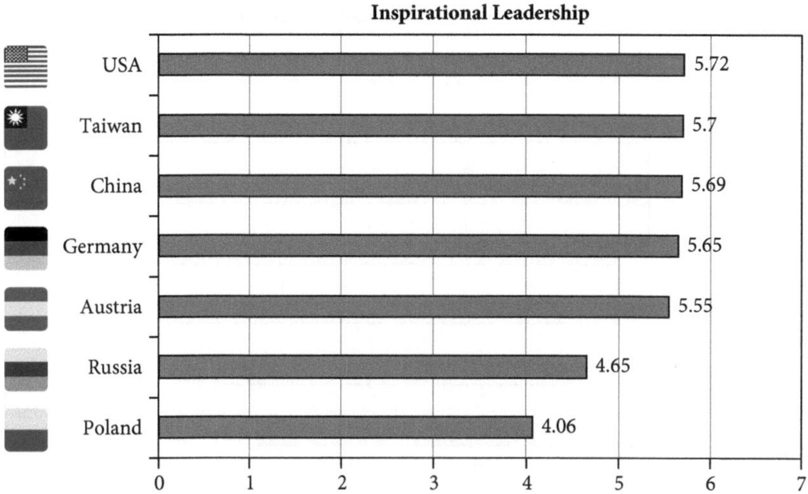

Fig. 1: Mean differences between investigated leaders on inspirational leadership dimension.

3 The inspirational leadership dimension

Under the GLOBE study, inspirational leadership expresses the ability to inspire, mobilize subordinates by giving courage, confidence, hope, praise, and to expect high work performance on the part of team members.

Fig. 1 displays the mean differences between CEOs and Polish middle managers with regard to the inspirational leadership dimension.

The research findings, displayed in Fig. 1, indicate that Russian CEOs and Polish middle managers contain significantly lower levels of inspirational leadership attributes than the leaders from the remaining countries. Based on the GLOBE research findings, it was empirically demonstrated that inspirational leadership behavior is concerned with the development of enthusiasm and dedication, by affecting strong emotions in regard to subordinates needs, values, dreams, and ideas.

Inspirational leadership behavior may appeal to subordinates' desire to feel important, to accomplish significant organizational goals, to perform an exceptional task, or to participate in a fascinating and inspiring one.

4 The visionary leadership dimension

Under the GLOBE project, visionary leaders inspire their followers with a highly ambitious vision, set high performance objectives, are well-organized, effectively

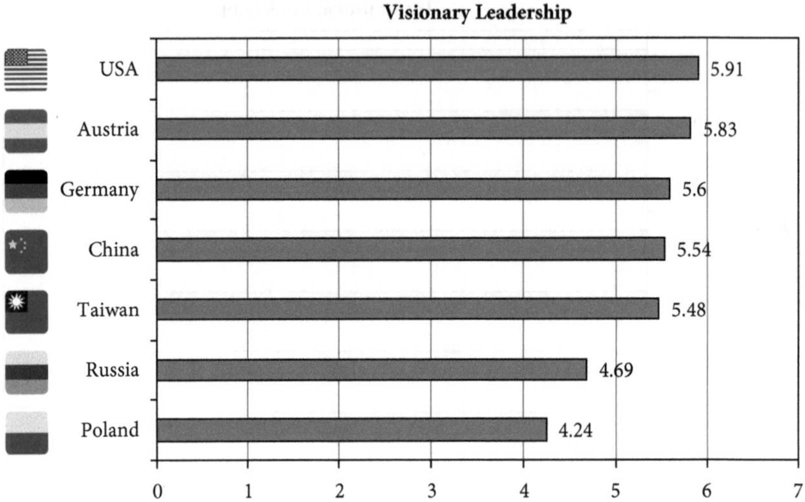

Fig. 2: Mean differences between investigated leaders on visionary leadership dimension.

manage their organizations, are likely to lead highly motivated teams, and create successful results for the organization.

Visionary leadership anticipates and prepares for an array of possible events. Important factors of visionary leadership are envisioning future events and providing long-term direction to subordinates. Thomas and Greenberger (1995) argued that the ability to create vision is to some extent associated with the future-time perspective characterized by the leader. A leader who is focused on future orientation has a clear picture of where the organization will be in a few years, and makes plans and directs his energy towards achieving future goals.

Fig. 2 displays the mean differences between the compared CEOs and Polish middle managers regarding the visionary leadership dimension.

The research results displayed in Fig. 2 demonstrate substantial evidence of differences in mean scores on visionary leadership between the compared groups of leaders. Russian CEOs and Polish middle managers display significantly lower levels of visionary leadership attributes than the remaining groups of managers.

Organizations that value future orientation demonstrate a tendency to endorse the effectiveness of visionary leadership. Hofstede (1991, 2000) postulated that long-term orientation is essential for a high tendency to save, while short-term orientation results in a tendency to enjoy leisure in the present time and emphasizes above all the immediate interests of the people.

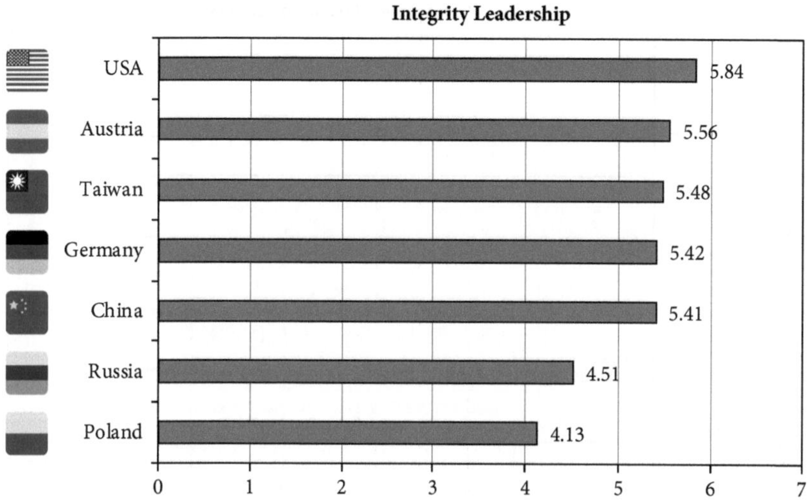

Fig. 3: Mean differences between investigated leaders on integrity leadership dimension.

Leaders who value vision have the ability to inspire and motivate subordinates to work hard in order to achieve organizational objectives.

5 The integrity leadership dimension

Integrity as a leadership dimension within the GLOBE project indicates leaders who are honest, and deserve to be trusted as they mean what they say and can be relied upon to keep their word. Their behavior is always ethical, and they express a strong sense of value and purpose, and behave accordingly.

Fig. 3 reports the mean differences between the analyzed groups of leaders on the integrity leadership dimension.

From a comparison of research findings under the GLOBE project, Phase 3, displayed in Fig. 3, it can be concluded that Russian CEOs as well as Polish middle managers score significantly lower on the integrity leadership dimension than leaders from the remaining countries.

Leaders demonstrating a high level of integrity are able to set an example, through their own behavior, for subordinates to stimulate enthusiasm and effort to perform tasks better. Such leaders are likely to influence motivation and satisfaction of their subordinates. As Yukl stated, "subordinates are usually more satisfied with a leader who is friendly and helpful, shows trust and respect, and demonstrates concern for their needs and feelings" (Yukl, 1994, p. 446).

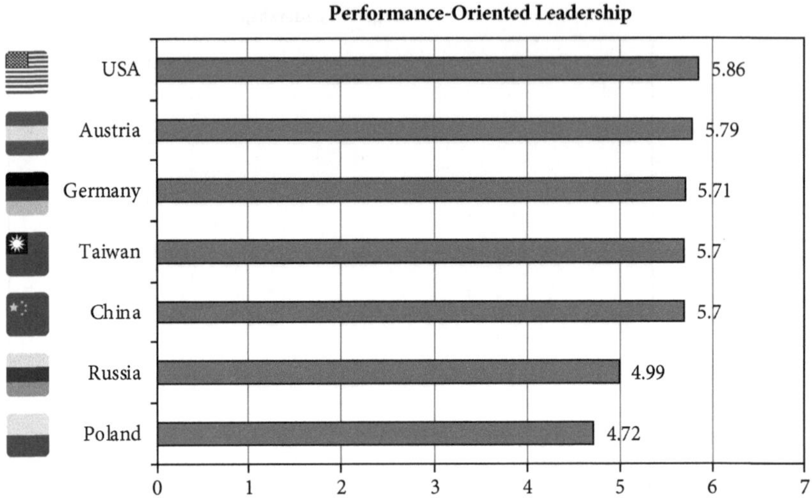

Fig. 4: Mean differences between investigated leaders on performance orientation.

6 The performance leadership dimension

Performance-oriented leaders are concerned with setting high standards, challenging goals, and high performance expectations. Such leaders work hard, and seek continuous improvement in performance (McClelland, 1987; Steers et al., 1996).

Fig. 4 presents the averaged ranking scores for the compared groups of leaders on performance orientation.

The research results shown in Fig. 4 indicate that Russian CEOs and Polish middle managers demonstrate significantly lower levels of performance orientation than the remaining groups of leaders. Based on the GLOBE research findings, societies whose members demonstrate strong performance orientation value education and learning, set high performance goals, and value expressing initiative (House et al., 2014; McClelland, 1987).

It is worth noting that the GLOBE research results on performance orientation showed that performance-oriented societies are more economically prosperous. Measures of economic health applied by GLOBE revealed a strong and significant correlation with three scales: "economic prosperity (correlation=.573, $p<.001$), public support for economic prosperity (correlation=.547, $p<.001$) and societal support for economic prosperity (correlation=.367, $p<.05$)" (House et al., 2004, p. 254).

It should be noted that Hofstede and Bond (1988) demonstrated that "Confucian Dynamism" was significantly correlated with economic growth among 22 societies under their investigation. Their concept of "Confucian Dynamism" has a strong connection with McClelland's need for achievement and GLOBE's performance orientation, lending support to the idea that societal and organizational practices that encourage achievement motivation are solutions to economic and business success. Peterson et al. (2003) discovered that the five dimensions of CEO personality (conscientiousness, emotional stability, agreeableness, extraversion, and openness) influence TMT dynamics, and TMT dynamics in turn are associated with firm performance.

The data presented in Figs. 5 and 6 indicate that CEOs are also reported (with the exception of Russian and Polish managers) to be generally team-oriented (5 out of 7 on a Likert scale) and participative (4.84 out of 7 on a Likert scale). CEOs in most investigated countries score around 5 on both dimensions.

7 The team-oriented leadership dimension

Team-oriented leaders are loyal to their followers and express care for the welfare of their team members. They use their authority and interpersonal skills to develop the team's internal dynamics and to build a cohesive working unit.

Fig. 5 presents the data associated with mean differences between CEOs and Polish middle managers on team-oriented leadership dimensions.

The results presented in Fig. 5 indicate that CEOs in all the investigated countries (with the exception of Russian CEOs and Polish middle managers) are reported to behave in generally team-oriented ways, scoring above 5 on a 7-point Likert scale. Under the GLOBE study, it was found that team-oriented leaders are concerned with expressing the importance of cooperation between team members for achieving organizational goals, as well as individual objectives. Numerous studies provide strong evidence that leaders' ability in team building is highly relevant for intensifying subordinates' identification with the organization's mission and leadership effectiveness (Peters and Austin, 1985; Tichy and Devanna, 1986).

8 The participative leadership dimension

Participative leaders express the view that subordinates have the potential to contribute to decision-making, and should be involved in the process and its implementation. They are also convinced that debate, discussion, and disagreement are natural parts of successful decision-making and should not be restrained. They give followers a high degree of discretion to perform work.

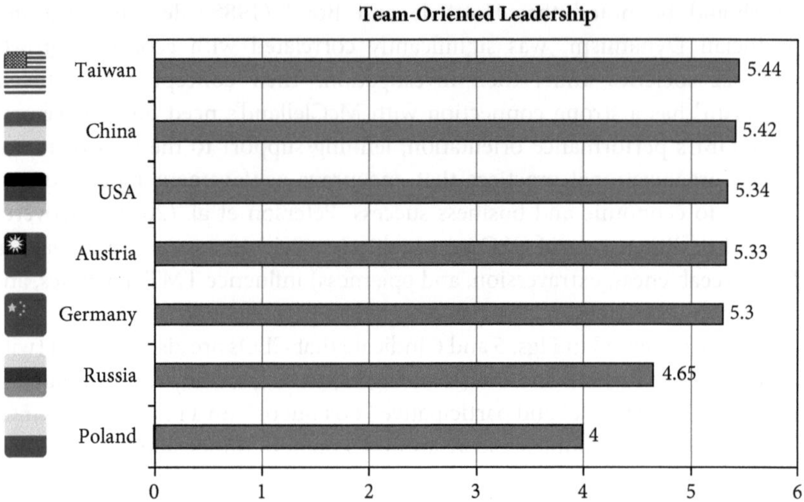

Fig. 5: Mean differences between investigated leaders on team-oriented leadership dimension.

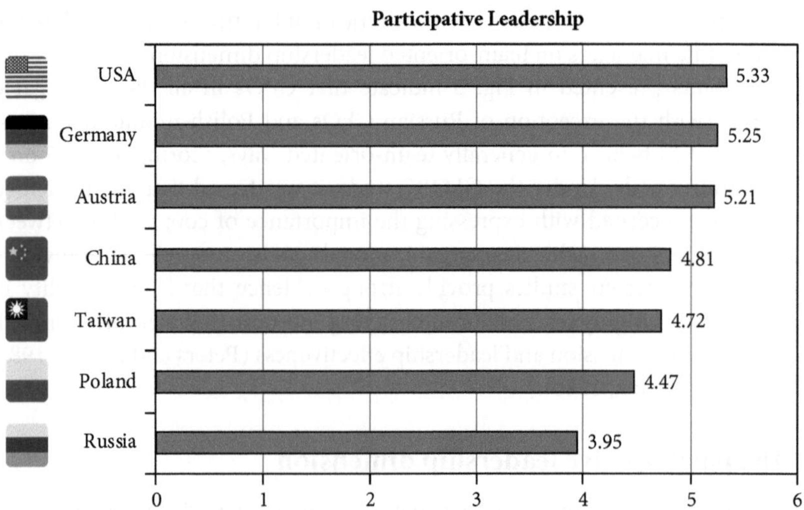

Fig. 6: Mean differences between investigated leaders on participative leadership dimension.

Fig. 6 displays the findings concerned with mean differences between CEOs and Polish middle managers on the participative leadership dimension.

The research findings presented in Fig. 6 indicate that participative leadership behavior is perceived to be more important in facilitating leadership effectiveness for the leaders in the United States, Germany, and Austria than for leaders in Russia, Poland, and partly for the leaders in Taiwan and China.

Another interesting finding emerges when considering participative leadership in its impact on subordinates' dedication to organizational goals. It turned out that participative behavior is positive in its effects on predicting TMT dedication ($r = .22$, $p < .01$), and the autocratic dimension is highly negative on predicting direct subordinates' dedication ($r = -.12$, $p < .01$) (House et al., 2014). Our research results point to the conclusion that the less a participative leadership style is applied towards subordinates, there is more opportunity to manifest autocratic leadership behavior.

It should be mentioned that Maczynski et al. (1994) conducted a cross-cultural study on leadership style among matched samples of Polish, Austrian, and American managers. The matching was done on the basis of those organizational and demographic factors known to influence leadership style: sex (Jago and Vroom, 1982), hierarchical level (Jago and Vroom, 1977), managerial function (Jago, 1980), and age (Jago, 1980). Ninety-one matched triads were established; managers within triads were similar in all aspects known to be associated with leadership behaviors, except for culture. Within each sample, the average age of respondents was 42 years. Four tested managers out of 91 respondents were female. Sixty-four percent of the sample performed the function of department head; twelve percent of respondents were executive managers. Thirty-four percent of the tested managers held production functions; thirty-eight percent of the sample described themselves as general managers. The framework of Vroom-Yetton (1973), and Bohnisch, Jago, and Reber (1987) was administered to explore differences among the leadership styles of the three cultures. Austrian managers were found to be the most participative, Polish managers the most autocratic, and American managers between the two.

It has been discovered that leadership style is influenced by the phenomenon of "Power Distance." Hofstede defines this concept as "the extent to which a society accepts the fact that power in institutions and organizations is distributed equally" (1980, p. 45).

Our research results revealed that "High power distance is dysfunctional since it discourages members of the society or organization from debate and voicing of divergent views. Asking questions may be regarded as criticizing and blaming, and therefore may not be allowed. In contrast within low power distance societies, the flexible distribution of power is expected to reinforce entrepreneurial innovation, broader participation in decision-making, and to restrain the abuse of power and corruption" (Mączyński et al., 2013, p. 15).

Under the GLOBE research, it has been found that nations which score lower on power distance of societal and organizational practices tend to be "more economically prosperous and competitively successful, enjoy higher levels of societal health, and human development" (House et al., 2004, p. 556). It can be assumed that progressing higher scores on power distance and autocratic leadership style for Polish managers produces unfavorable situations for Polish organizations relative to western institutions, and become particularly dysfunctional for organizational survival and effectiveness. We express the view that to be competitive with western organizations, Polish managers should acquire such values and leadership behavior which would help them to adapt to rapidly developing worldwide economic conditions (Mączyński et al., 1994; 1997; 2010; 2016a; Sułkowski, 2008; 2009).

9 Conclusions

In summary, our overall purpose in the present chapter was to compare a representative sample of Polish middle managers with a representative sample of CEOs from six chosen countries in regard to selected leadership attributes (traits and behaviors). The data presented in this chapter were drawn from a larger cross-cultural study of the GLOBE project, Phase 3, which was designed to investigate leadership attributes of CEOs from 24 countries (House et al., 2014). Poland did not participate in the GLOBE study, Phase 3, but nevertheless longitudinal research was conducted among 342 subordinates in regard to evaluations of traits and behaviors of their managers. The GLOBE, Phase 3 research is the first study to examine a large number (several thousands) of CEOs and senior executives in 24 countries, in order to empirically and directly investigate the relationship between culture and leadership attributes (traits and behaviors). We provide evidence that the investigated CEOs from the United States, Austria, Germany, China, and Taiwan (with the exception of Russian CEOs and Polish middle managers) are generally positively assessed by their direct staff in terms of inspirational, visionary, integrity, and performance-oriented leadership behaviors (constituents of charismatic leadership) and team-oriented behavior, as well as participative leadership.

Empirical research results under the GLOBE project, Phase 3, indicated that charismatic leadership behavior of CEOs has a huge influence on TMT dedication to organizational goals and are the most predictive of all leadership behaviors for TMT commitment. Team-oriented behavior of CEOs is the next most influential global leadership behavior. Participative leadership of CEOs was predictive for TMT dedication to organizational goals, but not firm competitive performance (House et al., 2014). It should be noted that research of Burke et al. (2006) has shown empirical evidence that there is a positive relationship between leader behaviors and team work performance.

Recent research by Wang, Tsui, and Xin (2011) indicated that CEOs' leadership behavior influences organizational performance and employees' attitudes. According to Hambrick (2007), the importance of leadership behavior at the top level of the organization is significant because CEOs influence not only the top level of management that directly reports to them, but also the larger organizational environment. In their earlier research, Hambrick and Mason (1984) concentrated on the role of demographic characteristics of CEOs on firm performance. These included such traits as age, functional path, formal education, and socioeconomic background. Nevertheless, the relationship between CEO demographic attributes and firm performance has found only limited support (Waldman, Javidan, and Varella, 2004).

A further review of the analyzed research results shows that CEOs in Russia and Polish middle managers show strong similarities. They tend to behave in less charismatic, team-oriented, and participative ways than the CEOs in the remaining countries. In addition, research results not portrayed in our chapter indicate a considerably less negative attitude towards autocratic leadership on the part of Russian and Polish managers in comparison to CEOs from the remaining countries.

Interpreting our findings in this light leads to the conclusion that profound developments in political and economic systems, particularly in Poland, are not sufficient conditions to potentially modify leadership behaviors and subsequent organizational practices. It would mean that deep changes in people's mentality are necessary to produce desirable conditions in cultural values and succeeding traits and behaviors (Hofstede 2000; 1991; 1980; Martan, 1993; Mączyński et al., 2009; 2013; 2016 a,b,c: Shabo et al., 1997).

It should be emphasized that under the current conditions in Poland, control no longer comes so exclusively from high-ranking leaders. Employees now have much more power and concurrent expectations that their preferences and interests will be taken into consideration. In other words, leaders can no longer behave effectively by applying an autocratic leadership style. Today, Polish organizations expect more participative leadership practices compatible with human capital conceptions of what participation signifies (Mączyński, 1996, 1998).

Research evidence accumulated by Hofstede (2000) and Maczynski et al. (1994) shows that there is a strong relationship between power distance and leadership style. Research results presented by Maczynski et al. (2009) demonstrate that power distance is still a persistent phenomenon deeply embedded in Polish culture, which has an intense influence on the leadership style of Polish managers. That is why Polish middle managers investigated in the period of 2008–2012 display a substantially less negative attitude towards autocratic behavior than their Western counterparts. The cross-cultural study conducted by Smith and Peterson (1988) revealed that in national cultures low in power distance, there is a greater reliance on participative decision making.

Research evidence accumulated by the first author of this chapter suggests that autocratic leadership syndrome can be broken through intensive training in participative leadership. Findings concerning the effects of decision participation training among Polish managers (Mączyński, 1996, 1998; Mączyński et al., 1997) offer hope for modification of organizational and management practices, to help Polish managers overcome dysfunctional leadership values and autocratic managerial styles in order to compete effectively with Western societies in a global business environment.

Research findings of the first author of this chapter clearly indicate that as a consequence of decision-participation training, the tendency to apply autocratic leadership styles decreased substantially, and that simultaneously a tendency to include followers in the decision-making process increased. This was expressed in a willingness to apply participative-decision styles (for example, group decision procedures) more frequently (Mączyński, 1996, 1998; Mączyński et al., 1997). It should be emphasized that the Vroom/Yetton (1973) and the Vroom/Jago (1988) models of decision-participation, and the method for assessing decision-making styles ("problem set," see Vroom, Yetton, and Jago, 1976; Mączyński, 1996, 1998), have significant educational value for leadership development. Decision-participation training encourages leaders to analyze their own managerial style more deeply so they would have a chance to appreciate the value of decision-participation training in the development of management effectiveness. Research findings concerning the positive effects of decision-participation training suggest that effective leadership style is an attribute possible to acquire, and that, among other factors, it can be modified through training.

Finally, it can be stated that research evidence presented in our chapter suggests that we have at our disposal cross-culturally validated, useful methods developed to diagnose the analyzed traits and behaviors responsible for leadership effectiveness and organizational performance. We hope that it will be found that our research findings are theoretically informative, and may have significant implications for improving leadership effectiveness.

References

Bass, B.M. (1990). *Bass and Stogdill's Handbook of Leadership: Theory, Research and Managerial Applications*. (*3rd ed.*) New York: Free Press.

Bohnisch, W., Jago, A.G., Reber, G. (1987). Zur interkulturellen Validitat des Vroom/Yetton 0 Modells. *Die Betriebswirtschaft*, *47*, 85–93.

Burke, C.S., Stagl, K.C., Klein, C., Goodwin, G.F., Salas, E., Halpin, S.M. (2006). What type of leadership behaviors are functional in teams? A meta-analysis. *Leadership Quarterly*, *17*, 288–307.

Den Hartog, D.N., Maczynski, J., Motowidlo, S.J., Jarmuz, S., Koopman, P.L., Thierry, H. Wilderom, C.P.M. (1997). Cross-cultural perceptions of leadership: A comparison of leadership and societal and organizational culture in The Netherlands and Poland. *Polish Psychological Bulletin*, *28*, 255–267.

Hambrick, D.C. (2007). Upper echelons theory: An update. *Academy of Management Review*, *32*(2), 334–343.

Hambrick, D.C., Mason, P.A. (1984). Upper echelons: The organization as a reflection of its top managers. *Academy of Management Review*, *9*(2), 193–206.

Hofstede, G. (1980). *Culture's Consequences: International Differences in Work-Related Values*. Beverly Hills: Sage.

Hofstede, G. (1991). *Cultures and Organizations: Software of the Mind*. London: McGraw-Hill.

Hofstede, G. (2000). *Kultury i organizacje. Zaprogramowanie umyslu*. Warszawa: Polskie Wydawnictwo Ekonomiczne.

Hofstede, G., Bond, M.H. (1998). The Confucius Connection: From cultural roots to economic growth. *Organizational Dynamics*, *16*(4), pp. 4–21.

House, R.J., Dorfman, P.W., Javidan, M., Hanges, P.J., Sully de Luque, M.F. (2014). *Strategic Leadership Across Cultures*. Thousand Oaks: SAGE Publications, Inc.

House, R.J., Hanges, P.J., Javidan, M., Dorfman, P.W., Gupta, V. (2004). *Culture, Leadership and Organizations. The GLOBE Study of 62 Societies*, Thousand Oaks: SAGE Publications, Inc.

House R.J., Hanges, P.J., Ruiz-Quintanilla, S.A. (1997). GLOBE: The global leadership and organizational behavior effectiveness research program. *Polish Psychological Bulletin*, *28*, pp. 215–254.

Jago, A.G. (1980). Organizational characteristics and participative decision making. *Proceedings of the 12th Annual Conference of the American Institute of Decision Sciences*, 334–336.

Jago, A.G., Maczynski, J. Reber, G. (1996). Evolving leadership styles?: A comparison of Polish managers before and after market economy reforms. Polish Psychological Bulletin, *27*, 107–115.

Jago, A.G., Vroom, V.H. (1977). Hierarchical level and leadership style. *Organizational Behavior and Human Performance, 18*, 131–145.

Jago, A.G., Vroom, V.H. (1982). Sex differences in the incidence and evaluation of participative leader behavior. *Journal of Applied Psychology, 67*, 776–783.

Maczynski, J. (1996). *Participation in Decision Making*. Warsaw: Polish Academy of Sciences Press.

Maczynski, J. (1998). *Diagnosing Decision Participation*. Warsaw: Polish Academy of Sciences Press.

Maczynski, J., Jago, A.G., Reber, G. Bohnisch, W. (1994). Culture and leadership styles: A comparison of Polish, Austrian and US managers. *Polish Psychological Bulletin, 25*, pp. 303–315.

Maczynski, J., Kwiatkowski, P., Arcimowicz, A. (1997). Changing leadership style through training in participative decision making: Application of managerial practices in Polish organizations. *Polish Psychological Bulletin, 4 (28)*, 333–341.

Maczynski, J., Lobodzinski, A., Wyspianski, D., Kwiatkowski, P. (2009). Differences in organizational practices and preferred leader attributes between Polish managers investigated in 1996/1997 and 2008/2009. *Polish Psychological Bulletin, 40*, 127–132.

Maczynski, J., Sulkowski, L., Chmielecki, M. (2016a). *Kulturowe zroznicowanie w zakresie cech i zachowan przywodczych*, [w:] *Wybrane dylematy w zarzadzaniu zasobami ludzkimi*, red. M. Stor, A. Fornalczyk, T. Listwan, PRESCOM, Wroclaw, 2016.

Maczynski, J., Sulkowski, L., Wyspianski, D., Chmielecki, M., (2016b) *Pomiar cech i zachowan przywodczych w kontekscie wartosci kultury organizacyjnej*, [w:] *Metody i techniki zarzadzania zasobami ludzkimi*, red. T. Listwan, L. Sulkowski, Warszawa, s. 65–86.

Maczynski, J., Sulkowski, L., Chmielecki, M., Zajaczkowska A. (2013). Longitudinal studies on traits and behaviors of Polish managers. *Journal of Intercultural Management, 1* (5), 5–17.

Martan, L. (1993). The necessary change of human mentality. *Organization and Management, 73*, 89–95.

McClelland, D.C. (1987). *Human Motivation*. Cambridge, UK: Cambridge University Press.

Peters, T.J. Austin, N. (1985). *A Passion for Excellence: The Leadership Difference*. New York: Random House.

Peterson, R.S., Smith, D.B., Martorana, P.V., Owens, P.D. (2003). The impact of chief executive officer personality on top management team dynamics: One mechanism by which leadership affects organizational performance. *Journal of Applied Psychology, 88*, 795–808.

Smith, P. B. Peterson, M.F. (1988). *Leadership Organizations and Culture.* London: Sage.

Smith, P. B. Peterson, M.F. Misumi, J. (1994). Event management and work team effectiveness in Japan, Britain, and the USA. *Journal of Occupational and Organizational Psychology, 67*, 33–43.

Steers, R.M., Porter, L.W. Bigley, G.A. (1996). *Motivation and Leadership at Work (6th ed.)*. New York: McGraw-Hill.

Sulkowski, L. (2008). *Empowerment methods in social project management.* Intercultural Management Studies, 3/2, pp. 241–246.

Sulkowski, L. (2009). Universal sources of hierarchy and power from the perspective of neoevolutionism. *Journal of Intercultural Management, 1* (2), 59–69.

Sulkowski, L. (2012). *Kulturowe procesy zarzadzania.* Warszawa: Difin.

Szabo, E., Jarmuz, S., Maczynski, J., Reber, G. (1997). Autocratic Polish versus participative Austrian leaders: More than a cliché? *Polish Psychological Bulletin, 3* (28), 279–291.

Thomas, M.A., Greenberger, D.B. (1985). The relationship between leadership and time orientation. *Journal of Management Inquiry, 4*, 272–292.

Tichy, N.M., Devanna, M.A. (1986). *The Transformational Leader.* New York: John Wiley.

Vroom, V.H. Jago, A.G. (1978). On the validity of the Vroom-Yetton model. *Journal of Applied Psychology, 63*, 151–162.

Vroom, V.H. Jago, A.G. (1988). The New Leadership: Managing Participation in Organizations. Englewood Cliffs: Prentice Hall.

Vroom, V.H. Yetton, P.W. (1973). *Leadership and Decision-Making.* Pittsburgh: University of Pittsburgh Press.

Vroom, V.H. Yetton, P.W. Jago, A.G. (1976). Problem Set #5. New Haven: Yale University, School of Organization and Management.

Waldman, D.A., Javidan, M., Varella, P. (2004). Charismatic leadership at the strategic level: A new application of upper echelons theory. *Leadership Quarterly, 15*, 355–381.

Wang, H., Tsui, A.S., Xin, K.R. (2011). CEO Leadership behaviors, organizational performance, and employees' attitudes. *Leadership Quarterly, 22*, 92–105.

Yukl, G. (1994). *Leadership in Organizations* (*3rd ed.*). Englewood Cliffs: Prentice Hall.

List of Illustrations

Dariusz Dolinski and Tomasz Grzyb
Social Influence in Management – Possibilities for Using the "Power of WE" in the Everyday Work of a Manager
Fig. 1: Six powers of social influence. 15

Werner Auer-Rizzi, Gerhard Reber, Jerzy Mączyński, Łukasz Prysiński, and Dariusz Wyspiański
Social Partnership: Comparisons between Managers in Four Countries Based on the Vroom/Yetton Model
Fig. 1: Mean Level of Participation of Skoda managers in comparison to other Czech and German managers. (Source: Auer-Rizzi & Reber, 2013, 23) 66

Sylwia Przytuła
Expatriate Leaders
Fig. 1: Global leaders in cultural context. Source: Dziatzko et al. (2016). 123
Fig. 2: Word cloud for "global leader". Source: www.wordle.net. 127
Fig. 3: Cloud of chosen terms of assigned expatriate in the literature of the subject. Source: McNulty, I., Brewster (2017). 129
Fig. 4: Word cloud for „expatriate". Source: www.wordle.net. 129
Fig. 5: Contemporary model of global leadership. Source: based on Steers et al. (2012, p. 480). 131
Fig. 6: Word cloud for expat leader's competencies. Source: www.wordle.net. 137
Fig. 7: Types of cross-border managers. Source: Cogin, Fish (2010). 138

Jerzy Mączyński and Łukasz Sułkowski
A Seven Nation Study of Leadership Attributes
Fig. 1: Mean differences between investigated leaders on inspirational leadership dimension. 155
Fig. 2: Mean differences between investigated leaders on visionary leadership dimension. 156
Fig. 3: Mean differences between investigated leaders on integrity leadership dimension. 157
Fig. 4: Mean differences between investigated leaders on performance orientation. 158

Fig. 5: Mean differences between investigated leaders on team-oriented leadership dimension. 160
Fig. 6: Mean differences between investigated leaders on participative leadership dimension. 160

List of Tables

Werner Auer-Rizzi, Gerhard Reber, Jerzy Mączyński, Łukasz Prysiński, and Dariusz Wyspiański
Social Partnership: Comparisons between Managers in Four Countries Based on the Vroom/Yetton Model
Tab. 1: Longitudinal analysis of leadership behaviour in Austria, Germany, Czech Republic, and Poland. 60

Łukasz Haromszeki and Tadeusz Listwan
Organisational Leaders in Public Institutions: Operating Amidst the Prevalent and Desirable Organisational Culture
Tab. 1: Opinions of organisational leaders in public institutions on the current (O-Hierarchy) organisational culture. Source: own study based on research 97
Tab. 2: Opinions of organisational leaders in public institutions on the desired future and ideal (P-Hierarchy) organisational culture. Source: own study based on research 97
Tab. 3: Opinions of organisational leaders in public institutions on the current (O-Adhocracy) organisational culture. Source: own study based on research 98
Tab. 4: Opinions of organisational leaders in public institutions about the desired future and ideal (P-Adhocracy) organisational culture. Source: own study based on research 98
Tab. 5: Opinions of organisational leaders in public institutions on the current (O-Market) organisational culture. Source: own study based on research 98
Tab. 6: Opinions of organisational leaders in public institutions on the desired future and ideal (P-Market) organisational culture. Source: own study based on research 99
Tab. 7: Opinions of organisational leaders in public institutions on the current (O-Clan) organisational culture. Source: own study based on research 100
Tab. 8: Opinions of organisational leaders in public institutions on the desired future and ideal (P-Clan) organisational culture. Source: own study based on research 100
Tab. 9: The sense of freedom of organisational leaders in public institutions and their preferences in the field of organisational culture. Source: own study based on research 101

Sylwia Przytuła
Expatriate Leaders
Tab. 1: Chosen definitions of a "global leader". Source: Mendenhall et al. (2012, p. 495) 126
Tab. 2: Chosen definition of an "assigned expatriate". Source: author's own work 128
Tab. 3: Key competencies of expatriate leaders. Source: own work based on literature review 135

Jerzy Mączyński and Łukasz Sułkowski
A Seven-Nation Study of Leadership Attributes
Tab. 1: Rank order of selected CEO leadership behaviors predicting top management team dedication and firm competitive performance. 154

About the Authors

Werner Auer-Rizzi is an associate professor of Business Administration at the Institute for Organization Science at Johannes Kepler University Linz and the Director of the Joint Master Program Global Business. He studied Business Administration and Informatics and worked as a software developer during his studies. Before joining the Institute for International Management Studies at Johannes Kepler University in 1988, he worked as a system analyst with IBM, White Plains, New York and on several projects in Belgium (Ford) and Norway (Statoil). He received his Doctoral degree in 1992 and the "Habilitation" for Business Administration in 1998. He spent one year as a visiting scholar at the Rotman School of Management of the University of Toronto in 1997 and has been a guest professor at the Turku School of Economics every year since 2000. In 2007 the course "Culture and International Management", taught together with Dr. Michael Berry, was awarded by the Finnish Association of Management Graduates as "the best intercultural course in Finland". In December 2007, he was appointed Adjunct Professor at the Turku School of Economics. Werner's teaching and research is grounded in the field of Organizational Behavior. His current research interests include cross-cultural and international aspects of management and leadership, and trust in organizations. He is devoted to creating intercultural learning environments for students in cooperation with universities around the world.

Michał Chmielecki, PhD is an independent management consultant. He works for clients from Fortune 500 and Rzeczpospolita 100 lists. He is an assistant professor at Clark University (USA) and the University of Social Sciences (Poland). His areas of expertise include international negotiations and cross-cultural management. He serves as the associate editor of the Journal of Intercultural Management and the editor of the Entrepreneurship and Management Journal.

Dariusz Doliński – professor, social psychologist, earned his Ph.D. in 1988 from the social psychology program at Warsaw University. He works for the Wroclaw Faculty of the Warsaw School of Social Psychology (Poland), and is the president of the Polish Society for Social Psychology, past president of the Committee for Psychology of the Polish Academy of Sciences, past member of the Editorial Board of Social Influence, editor of Polish Psychological Bulletin, and is the author of 12 books and over 250 articles and book chapters. He is working in the field of social influence.

Tomasz Grzyb, PhD is an assistant professor at SWPS University of Social Sciences and Humanities in Wrocław, Poland, and a visiting lecturer in NATO School in Germany. His main areas of interest are social influence and manipulation techniques. He is also a supporter of courses concerning the basics of social influence studies organized for military officers engaged in PSYOPS. He has published a number of articles about marketing, social psychology, advertising, and education.

Łukasz Haromszeki is an assistant professor in the Human Resources Management Department at Wroclaw University of Economics, an interdisciplinary educated HRM expert – Master in Management (2002) and Doctor of Economics (2007) from Wroclaw University of Economics, Postgraduate Studies of Philosophy and Ethics (2004) and Management Psychology (2012), University of Wroclaw, School of Human Rights (2005), Helsinki Foundation for Human Rights, Postgraduate Studies of Leadership and Social Communication (2002), Military University of Technology in Warsaw, English Language and Psychology Courses (1999), Diablo Valley College San Ramon, CA. His research interests include: organizational leadership, management by values and CSR, Strategic HRM, and influencing and motivating people. Since 2005 he has been conducting studies about various dimensions of leadership in local communities, the research of talented leaders in three sectors of the Polish economy (presented at the IHRM Conference at Penn State University in 2013), a study of expectations towards leaders (qualifications and competences, style of leadership, etc.) in the regional scope (CEE countries) in the context of a global perspective. He has conducted a study for the higher doctor's degree thesis *Local leaders as an example of organizational leaders in civil society* from 2014 to 2016. Since 2017 he has been a co-investigator in a project financed by the National Science Center, Poland. He is also the Head of Human Resources Management Postgraduate Studies and Coordinator of the Executive MBA Program at Wrocław University of Economics. He is also a member of The Youth Team in the Polish Academy of Sciences and an expert/auditor in HRM Leader Award, the Institute of Labor and Social Studies. He is the author and co-author of over 90 scientific articles and specialist documents. Since 2007 he has been a consultant, lecturer, and tutor in educational and investment projects, mostly co-financed by the European Union. He is an expert in Programs – Interreg Central Europe, Regional Operational Programme for the Lower Silesian, Pomeranian and Silesian Voivodships in the fields of, e.g., Enterprise and Employees' Adaptation, SME's Employees' Competences and Qualifications, Education, Employment and Regional Development. He conducts lectures and classes in both Polish and English (over 30 subjects for Bachelor's, Master's, and Postgraduate's students).

Tadeusz Listwan is a professor of management. His primary scientific and research interest is human resource management, in particular with regard to the managerial staff in organizations. He is the author or co-author of over 220 publications, including 30 books. He has extensive experience in empirical research, consulting, and training, especially in the area of the selection and development of managers. He is a long-time member of various scientific bodies, including the Committee on Organization and Management Sciences of the Polish Academy of Sciences. He has promoted 15 doctors of management sciences.

Jerzy Mączyński is a professor of Organizational Behavior at the University of Social Sciences in Poland. Prof. Mączyński is a highly active and productive social science scholar, whose major interests concern managerial effectiveness and management problems associated with the conversion of Poland's previously centralized economy to a free market economy. In total, he has published 140 articles and seven books concerning these topics. Additionally he edited eight English-language scientific journals. Furthermore, not only is Prof. Mączyński highly productive, his work meets high standards of scholarly quality. Professor Mączyński served as Visiting Professor at several universities in the United States and Western Europe. Among others, he was invited by the University of Toledo (US), University of Florida (US), University of Nottingham (UK), University of Westminster (UK), University of Linz (Austria), University of Amsterdam (Netherlands), University of Nancy (France), the Swedish School of Economics (Finland). As a result of these professorships he has developed scientific cooperation with several of the universities.

Łukasz Prysiński – PhD, financial advisor, specializes in the restructuring and optimization of business processes, personal development coach. He is a graduate of Warsaw School of Economics and University of Łódź. He specializes in the optimization of: the financial and economic condition of companies, management processes, motivating systems, personal and professional development. He gained experience as a director of the MBA program, director of an employers' association, president of a foundation and board of directors member, coach and trainer. He is the author of publications in the field of financial analysis, investment appraisal, and the efficiency of industry. He also participates in many international conferences. He teaches Financial Analysis and Managerial Accounting at Polish and foreign universities.

Sylwia Przytuła PhD Professor at the Wroclaw University of Economics and University of Social Sciences, her research and scientific interests are: expatriation, international HRM, cultural differences in global business. She is a member of

SIETAR Poland (Society for Intercultural Education, Training and Research), HEF, and IMISCOE (International Migration, Integration and Social Cohesion). Author and co-author of 130 of scientific publications, and reviewer of International Journal of HRM, Journal of Organizational Change Management. She participated in numerous international scholarships for academics in top European Universities (DCU, UCM, Erasmus University, Aalborg University, Malaga University, University of Applied Sciences Mainz , Porto University, ESCIP School of International Business , ESADE, in the USA (Carnegie Mellon University, Pennstate University) and China (Renmin University).

Gerhard Reber was born in 1937 in Mannheim, Germany. He studied Business Administration at the Universities in Mannheim (Wirtschaftshochschule, now Universität Mannheim) and Munich (Ludwig Maximilian Universität), graduated with the title "Diplomkaufmann" in 1962, and was hired as a teaching and research assistant in the newly founded "Institute for Personnel". This institute, founded in 1963 by Professor August Marx, was an innovation in the area of Business Administration. As a student, Reber spent the summers working in Finland and Canada. These experiences – working for Marx and abroad – shaped his international professional career, which included integration of the social sciences and business administration. He received his Doctorate from the University of Mannheim in 1965, an MBA from the University of Toronto in 1966, and completed his "Habilitation" at the Hochschule für Wirtschafts- und Sozialwissenschaften in Linz, Austria (today: Johannes Kepler University) in 1973. In Linz he began his career in the same year, immediately after the Habilitation, as Full Professor for Organizational Behavior. In subsequent years he served his institution also as co-founder and subsequent head of the Foreign Language Department (1983–2005) and was involved in developing exchange programs for students (ERASMUS) with 15 European countries (1994–1995). Based on this experience, he turned his attention to creating exchange programs in North America and – after the liberation – countries in eastern Europe. From 1993–1997 he served as Dean of the Faculty of Social Sciences. For the Social Partners in Upper Austria, he founded the executive program LIMAK (Linz Management Akademie) in 1989 in cooperation with Emory University in Atlanta, the University of Toronto, and USW (a private business school in Germany) and continued as the academic head of LIMAK until 2005. After 2005, the year of his official retirement from the university, he continued working in an international three-university program of the Gustavson School of Business of the University of Victoria, the College of Management of the National Sun Yat-Sen University of Taiwan, and the Faculty of Social Sciences of the JKU in

Linz on the level of MBA students, until 2012. He was a visiting professor at the University of Dallas, Texas, in 1978, at the University of Toronto in 1982, and at the Business School of Emory University in Atlanta from 1987 to 1988. He has honorary doctorates from the University of St. Gallen, Switzerland, the Turku School of Economics in Finland, and the Linguistic University of Nischnij Nowgorod in Russia. From 1977 until 2002 he was co-editor of the German journal "Die Betriebswirtschaft". His teaching concentrated on social sciences within the area of business administration, this resulting in over a hundred publications. His special focus became the area of intercultural differences in leadership behavior. This was achieved with the help of a productive team, including the colleagues Wolf Böhnisch, Werner Auer-Rizzi, Erna Szabo, Artur Jago, Evelyne Glaser, and Jerzy Maczynski. Many thanks for this cooperation.

Czesław Sikorski PhD, Professor of the Department of Management in the Faculty of Management, University of Lodz, of which he was a director in the years 1999–2012. In his research activities he has been dealing with social aspects of management for many years, in particular, the aspects of organizational culture and organizational behaviour. He is the author of 23 books devoted to this subject, a co-author of 15 books and wrote 140 scientific articles and chapters in collective works. Between 1981 and 1987 he was the deputy dean of the Faculty of Economics and Sociology, and between 1996 and 1999, the deputy dean of the Faculty of Management at the University of Lodz. From 1993 to 1996 he was a member of the Committee on Organization and Management Sciences of the Polish Academy of Sciences. He was a member of an international team that prepared the program and conducted training of healthcare managers in the European Union as part of the EU Europhamili program from 2001 to 2003. In addition to scientific and didactic activities, Prof. Cz. Sikorski has many years of experience in consulting, especially regarding the selection of management staff. Between 1988 and 2000 he was the head of the team of experts in the Human Resources Consulting Office "Orgman".

Łukasz Sułkowski – Polish professor of economic sciences, specializing in management sciences. Currently employed in the Institute of Public Affairs of the Jagiellonian University, vice-president for international affairs of the Polish Accreditation Committee and Director of Clark University Branch Campus at University of Social Sciences in Poland. He is also the president of PCG Polska. Head of the Chair of Management of Higher Education Institutions at the Jagiellonian University, professor at Clark University, and University of Social Sciences. Since 2008 he has been editor-in-chief of the Journal of Intercultural Management "(DeGruyter). In 2004–2011 the editor-in-chief of "Organizacja i

Kierowanie" quarterly of the Committee of Organization and Management of the Polish Academy of Sciences "Organization and Management". Author or co-author of more than 300 publications, including 14 monographs published by such publishing houses as Springer, Lexington, Palgrave, Emerald, Lang, PWN, PWE. Project manager or coordinator of 16 EU research grants (e.g., 6th Framework Programme, EQUAL), National Science Centre, Ministry of Science and Higher Education and State Committee for Scientific Research. He currently manages the "UNIFUT" project of the University of the Future and Organizational improvement of the university of the future "("Dialogue", Ministry of Science and Higher Education). Member of four international research associations (AAM, EURAM, IFERA, PGV). Since 2014 member of the Committee for Culture and Media Management of the Polish Academy of Arts and Sciences (PAU), Committee for Culture and Media Management (PAU). Chairman of cyclical conferences "Family Business. Managing Family Companies" (7 editions), "Intercultural Management Congress" (11 editions). Promoter of 14 PhD dissertations at five universities. Reviewer in several dozen professorial, habilitation, and doctoral proceedings.

Dariusz Wyspiański – Psychologist, Certified Coach (Business & Life), Business Trainer, Manager with 25 years of experience in HR and Training Business Areas (Banking, IT , Industry, Consulting). Postgraduate studies – Technical University in Wrocław (*Management and Organization*), University of Wroclaw (*Psychology of Management*), Institute of Transactional Analysis, Cambridge, England (*Transactional Analysis Practitioner Certificate*). Academic lecturer (University of Social Sciences, Poland), co-author of scientific articles and books concerning leadership and management. Business Consultant, Founder of "Solution Brief Focused School of Coaching". Other areas of professional activity: Psychotherapy (*Certificate of World Association for Positive Psychotherapy* – Wiesbaden, Germany) and sports psychology (coaching and mental preparation).

New Horizons in Management Sciences

Edited by Lukasz Sulkowski

Vol. 1 Lukasz Sulkowski: Neodarwinism in Organization and Management. 2012.

Vol. 2 Lukasz Sulkowski: Epistemology of Management. 2013.

Vol. 3 Barbara Kożuch / Zbysław Dobrowolski: Creating Public Trust. An Organisational Perspective. 2014.

Vol. 4 Konrad Raczkowski / Lukasz Sulkowski (eds.): Tax Management and Tax Evasion. 2014.

Vol. 5 Michał Chmielecki / Łukasz Sułkowski: Metaphors in Management – Blend of Theory and Practice. 2017.

Vol. 6 Łukasz Sułkowski (ed.): Management and Culture of the University. 2017.

Vol. 7 Barbara Kożuch / Łukasz Sułkowski (eds.): Reflections about Contemporary Management. 2017.

Vol. 8 Łukasz Sułkowski/Ewa Grandys (eds.): New Challenges in Change Management. 2018.

Vol. 9 Zuzana Bačíková(ed.): Marketing in the Digital Era. 2018.

Vol. 10 Łukasz Sułkowski / Jerzy Mączyński / Sylwia Przytuła (eds.): Leadership across Cultures. 2019.

www.peterlang.com